T. K. Hervey

Rest on the Cross

T. K. Hervey

Rest on the Cross

ISBN/EAN: 9783337300340

Printed in Europe, USA, Canada, Australia, Japan

Cover: Foto ©Lupo / pixelio.de

More available books at **www.hansebooks.com**

REST, ON THE CROSS.

BY

ELEANORA LOUISA HERVEY,

AUTHOR OF "OUR LEGENDS AND LIVES," "THE FEASTS OF CAMELOT,"
"MY GODMOTHER'S STORIES FROM MANY LANDS," ETC., ETC.

"Pain thee not each crooked to redress,
The wrestling of this world asketh a fall;
Here is no home, here is but wilderness:
Forth, Pilgrim!
Look up on high, and thank thy God of all."
                                    CHAUCER.

LONDON:
R. WASHBOURNE, 18 PATERNOSTER ROW.
1877.

CONTENTS.

PART I.

CHAPTER	PAGE
I. EARLY YEARS	7
II. THE FORMALIST	15
III. ALICE BRUCE	24
IV. THE ANNOUNCEMENT	32
V. THE ARRIVAL	42
VI. THE CLIFF	50
VII. THE DEATH-BED	63
VIII. A COMMUNICATION	71
IX. THE AVOWAL	79
X. DESOLATION	89

PART II.

I. THE STRANGER	101
II. THE MEETING	113
III. THE "LOWER DEEP"	123
IV. THE PORTICO	133
V. THE PESTILENCE	140
VI. THE LOFT	151

CHAPTER	PAGE
VII. THE LOST FOUND	161
VIII. THE "GOING OUT OF EGYPT"	168
IX. A NIGHT AT SEA	180
X. HOMEWARD BOUND	192

PART III.

I. MAYBROOK	207
II. THE POOR RELATION	216
III. THE LORD OF THE MANOR	233
IV. DISUNION	241
V. A DISASTROUS DAY	250
VI. PARTING SCENES	261
VII. ROME	270
VIII. THE COMMUNION OF SOULS	278
IX. REST, ON THE CROSS	286

REST, ON THE CROSS.

CHAPTER I.

EARLY YEARS.

" The child is father of the man."—WORDSWORTH.

SHOULD these lines ever meet the eyes of the young when the hand that has traced them lies powerless, let me hope that the feelings they develop, and the struggles they depict, may not be without their use.

To the more mature this brief history will not be wholly unsuggestive. While to those newer to the world and its startling and strange truths—" stranger than fiction "—these deeply-shadowed pictures may possibly seem unlike the existing and breathing realities of life they represent, there are many among the elder wayfarers in its rugged paths who will behold, in such portraiture, the sterner features of their own past fortunes limned anew ;

and, as one life, however varied in its scenes and outward acts, is, in its more essential and internal character, but the reflex of all—the same series of hope and disappointment, passion and feeling, joy and grief—that which has been thought and felt, done and suffered, in the narrow compass of one human existence, may well find an echo in the being of another.

Nor is the voice less impressive because it reaches us out of the silence and darkness of the earth. The lips of the dead may speak truth to the living; and the lesson thus conveyed out of the dust into the upper air of a moving and breathing world, may spread an influence abroad which shall sink deep into the awakened sense—like those Eastern flowers that rise up through the perforated slabs that cover the Moslem graves, springing from corruption but giving out sweetness.

The period of childhood is, perhaps, that of all others to which the generality of men recur with most pleasure. This may arise from various causes. It is a time of almost perfect purity in thought and action; and thus offers to the mind, as a green field does to the eye, a relief from the contemplation of less pure, less peaceful, and more stirring objects. Or it may be that their very indistinctness lends a charm to its recollections, giving scope for the imagination to invest every circumstance, however trifling, with fictitious colours. More probably still, this yearning feeling towards the budding time of the human plant may arise from the subsequent withering of its blossoms, and the blighting or decaying of its fruit ; for who ever looked back with emotion upon the period of his childhood, until the prospect before him was a blank ?

What childhood is to the memory of man, the dawn of womanhood is to that of woman. To her all that is bright in imagination and fancy, all that is fresh and incommunicable in feeling, is connected with this first expanding of the soul under new aspects and new influences. It is as if the life which had gone before belonged to a different state of being, and the mortal creature suddenly became immortal, and all things—the very world itself—were born anew. It is the abasing of the clay, and the exalting of the spirit. It is the removing of the earth to make way for the foundation of a sacred column, raised by some master-hand and dedicated to the Divine.

Of my earlier years my recollections are, for the most part, vague and characterless.

The inquiring spirit, natural to most children, was not inactive in myself individually. So great indeed was my pertinacity in gathering information, and so acute were the conclusions I drew from all I heard, that it is probable I should have been chidden for the former habit, had not the latter proved a source of amusement to my instructors.

That in after years I did not benefit more by this early thirst for the acquisition of knowledge, is to be attributed to the nature and subjects of my inquiries. The beautiful, the graceful only, not the useful, had charms for my undiscerning eye; nature, to the exclusion of art, held undivided empire over my understanding; and what was good and pure alone found its way into my heart. The lily which lay couched upon the bosom of the water was a thing to be gazed at till the sense of sight grew weary, while the useful rushes on its banks were left to wave and rustle in the breeze, unnoticed, till the better-taught child of the poor basket-maker should seize them as its prize. The silkworm was not an indirect source of the wealth of nations, a little field-labourer in the cause of improvement and civilisation; but a creature whose business it was to feed upon the green leaves of the mulberry-tree beneath which I played ; to weave a silken habitation, and, in process of time, rise, a winged creature, from its seeming tomb. The companions with whom I played, if they did what was right and approved, and were in grief, I wept over ; but if they were in fault, I turned away from them. There was love enough in my pity, but not pity enough in my love.

This want of toleration for the frailties of others is owing, later in life, to an exaggerated, or rather to a half-sided view of both virtue and vice. The finer shades, the gradual melting of one tint into another, is not sufficiently considered in our contemplation of the pictures presented to us in our intercourse with the world. In the alchymy of the mind, as in the science of which it is a type, we employ a furnace to transmute the materials upon which we work. The instant the coarser metal ceases to present its original properties, the alchymist exclaims, "Behold, it is gold!" In other words, the moment vice ceases to appear such, the imagination transforms it into virtue; and conversely. Children sometimes, without reasoning, act in a similar manner from impulse. I was the child of impulse, and I did so.

What wonder then that, young and innocent,

forming to myself a world of which the boundary line of good and evil was thus strongly marked, I should, at the very first outset in life, engage too enthusiastically in the cause of virtue ; that I should hold up to imitation all that was sublime in meditation and heroic in action ; and that thus a rule of conduct should be laid down which could scarcely be adapted to the practice of life, and which, even if it could by possibility be carried into action, must necessarily produce results calculated to sicken with disappointment the quick spirit in whose depths it was conceived and perfected?

The one to whom I first directed the uncontrolled impulses of a warm and loving heart, and towards whom no excess of devotion could be misplaced, was my mother. Here the tricks of imagination were needed not. No power of the fancy was required to heighten the loveliness of her pure and perfect character, or to increase the strength of that natural tie which bound to her the affections of her child.

Even now, at this distance of time, I recall vividly to remembrance the intensity of terror which seized me, upon the occasion of the only illness I had ever known her to suffer from, and when first the possibility of her loss was presented to my mind. Little as I then knew of death, or of the mysterious connection between soul and body, it was enough to be told that, in dying, she would go from me; that I should see her no more—her—my mother, my second self, my all in the world; that I should never again throw myself into her arms, or shed my tears upon her bosom. It was not to be conceived—not to be thought of.

When the attempt was made to prepare me for the event hourly anticipated by all, my first feeling was anger against those who seemed to me instrumental in bringing about this work of dread, this fearful separation, this rending of limb from limb, and heart from heart. Vain were all precautions to exclude me from the sick-room. I burst from those around me in a paroxysm of passion, and took the first opportunity that offered of rushing into the room and up to the bed where my mother lay. Flinging my arms round her neck, I buried my face in her pillow. My tears were gone. The throbbings of my pulse were stilled. I held her; and she was safe.

Beautiful—beautiful faith in a child's young heart! Why has it not the power to perform the miracles of which it dreams; to stay the progress of disease; to snatch what it loves from the grave; and draw out the venom from the sting of death!

For this time the storm passed over without destroying. The prayers of the innocent, unuttered, but audible to the ear of the Most High, were heard.

When the stroke did fall, long afterwards, and when I was in my twelfth year, it was alike without anticipation and without warning. A paralytic seizure, producing almost instant death, robbed me of her who was dearest to me on the earth.

When it is considered that I was an only child nursed in the fulness of affection, and seeking and finding my only happiness at her side, words must be faint to speak the utter desolation of heart under which I was now to sink. Deprived long since by death—as I then believed—of a father's care; without sister of brother to satisfy my longings for a love like that which was taken away; and ill formed by disposition and early habits to find sympathy in the world, I felt orphaned in a double sense, and, as has been emphatically said, "thrown upon the Fatherhood of God."

CHAPTER II.

THE FORMALIST.

"Such the religion of a mind that steers
  Its way to bliss between its hopes and fears;
  Whose virtues all their stated limits know,
  Like well-dried herbs that neither fade nor grow."
                                                    CRABBE.

AMONG the negative influences by which my character was formed, one of the most important, whether for good or for evil, was that of my not having received a school education. Although such a discipline would in all probability have tended greatly to correct that exuberance of imagination and abandonment of feeling for which I was remarkable; yet I am inclined to think that, on the whole, the advantages derived from it would have been more than counterbalanced by the habits and tones of thought which, if not directly inculcated, are too often the result of the system of female education as conducted in public schools.

In entering upon this kind of training, a girl passes the threshold of that home by whose hearth she has been reared, and within whose bounds her first ideas have been instilled through the medium of the affections, and she is suddenly thrown, with all her home-love full upon her, into the crowded schoolroom, amidst strange companions, and under the eye of a strange instructor. Here her heart receives its first chill. Here the hardening process of the world upon the soft clay of youth is first begun. Her feelings are not given her to be indulged here. If she weeps for the familiar face and the beloved voice of old, she meets with no sympathy, but a grave rebuke. If household thoughts press too vividly upon her, so as to distract her attention from the tedious routine of duties—almost wholly unrelieved by any beneficial exercise of either mind or body—which is imposed on her, she is subjected to a still harsher reprimand. And what is the result? She either loses her elasticity of mind, and, as a natural consequence, sinks into ill health, when she is at length recalled to the home from which she has been torn, and which she ought never to have quitted; or the other, and more frequent state of things take place—she becomes a convert to what she contemned;

she enters into quarrels; practises deceit in eluding the tasks appointed her; indulges in idle conversations; and begins to think she is becoming very comfortable. And now, instead of looking to home as the sacred refuge—the sanctuary of her soul, she finds "there is a world elsewhere." In short, she has become thoroughly school-bred.

In a home education all is widely different. Whether conducted solely under the eye of a parent, or with the assistance of a governess, this is, of all others, the method best adapted to the culture of that delicate plant—woman. Her intellectual progress is not here forced by the mill-wheel of tyrannical government. Her affections are fostered at the same time that her mental powers are strengthened; and while the blood flows in an equal current, quickened into healthful circulation by the exercise of all her faculties, the balance of mind and body preserves its just equipoise; and, supposing her to be endowed with a disposition so happily constituted as to derive the full benefit of the influences directed towards its development her nature then attains the highest perfection of which it is capable.

On the death of my mother, to whom I owed all the good that entered into my composition,

I was at once transferred to the care of the eldest of my maternal aunts. Although a person who, in her own opinion, exercised an important influence, both by precept and example, in her own immediate neighbourhood, yet so perverse were the principles upon which she acted, and so constantly were her efforts to inculcate lessons of piety counteracted by the method she took to impart them, that it would have been difficult to say what real good she did, or what specific purpose she fulfilled in the scale of being. She was one of those who are content to " act religion instead of doing it." Her love—if indeed she could ever condescend to love what she termed " corrupt humanity"— was not heart-warm; there was no pulse of life in it. Her charity was the mere charity which ministers to the wants of the body, while it leaves those of the mind uncared for; and in this her means would not allow her to indulge. That a generous sympathy for the distress of the afflicted generally, and a forbearance even towards those who are sufferers from the consequences of their own evil passions, were necessary portions of the creed she professed, seemed never to have occurred to her. If she visited the sick, she left the cottage of the labourer more desolate than she found it; for she gave only that of which the heart of the sufferer was full—prayer; while she took away that of which it was most barren—hope, the twofold hope of the sinned against and sinning, the hope of sympathy on earth and of mercy in heaven. If she entered the Sunday-school, it is true that the children were awed by her presence, that they put on a graver aspect, and lifted up their little voices in the Sabbath-song of praise with a more solemn intonation; but the image of the Deity in their minds was in a moment transformed from a God of love to a God of fear, by the sudden apparition of this—to them—severe herald of His displeasure.

In her own household the same cold, harsh measures were pursued. For the house itself, a gloom seemed to rest on everything, animate and inanimate, within its walls. And as for the servants—God help them! I pitied them from my heart. Like the inhabitants of Chorasm, they were driven to worship with the scourge. Not only their actions, but their words, their looks, their dress—nay, if possible, their very thoughts, were ruled over with a strictness of supervision that would have done honour to an Inquisitor.

My aunt Clinton, or, I should say simply,

Dorothea—for so she chose to be addressed, because, as she said, it reminded her that she was the "Gift of God"—and after whom I had been christened Dora, was at this time verging towards her seventieth year, and a widow. With an unprepossessing person, and manners so frigid, it was a matter of wonder that my aunt should ever have married. This was as little conceivable as that she should ever have been young.

And here, in spite of what she was, a touch of compassion mingles with the thought of what she had been. There must have been a time when this iron frame wore the softness of youth; when the eye that now dealt terror, could melt into tenderness, and impart the blest assurance of affection; when the lip which for many a year had been attuned only to severity, had uttered tones of gentleness; and when the heart, now closed to every kindly impression, and withered and dried up into a lifeless husk, had been filled to overflowing with all those wholesome juices, those feeders of its inmost core, which are the life-sap of humanity —hope and joy, love and pity, gratitude and adoration.

Such we are, and such does life make us. The moral change which takes place during the progress from infancy to age ; the loss of the vital warmth of youth beneath the chilling atmosphere of the world, followed by the gradual appearance of those harsher and more crude materials which go to the full completion of the human being, and which, though latent, are but slowly developed, is somewhat analogous to the formation of substances from the waters of boiling springs. As long as these retain their heat, the lime and flint contained in them is not apparent ; but when exposed to the air till that heat is lost, they then, by slow degrees, and in minute particles, deposit these substances, and form incrustations of them in their way from the fountain.

It might naturally be supposed that, thrown thus early under the dominion of so formidable a character, I should either become imbued with views and ideas similar to those daily presented to me ; or that my mind, in exercising an uniform rebellion against the dictates of so harsh a philosophy, would, by a natural reaction, be led into irreligion and scepticism. But neither was the case.

To guard me against the former error, the image of my lost mother, with all her meek and gentle piety, her suffering love, her heavenly charity, ever rose up visibly before me ;

and I could no more turn my faith away from the God of peace and pardon in whose likeness she was framed, than I could cease to cherish her example, or to love and reverence her, even in the grave.

On the other hand, I was too young to enter into anything like religious controversy; therefore, the only effect produced by the rigid forms of worship—for they were forms only—which were depicted as the one great duty, the aim and end of existence, was that of making me shrink more and more within myself—to wonder and be silent. For to suppose that any communion of feeling could by possibility exist between two natures so totally opposed, were to infer a kind of miracle. Each continued to preserve as distinct an identity as those rivers which may sometimes be observed to join their streams, but whose junction is marked by diversity of colour. We might meet, but never mingle.

Still it was to be feared that this too constant turning of the mental eye inwardly upon self, might make me less social, and more timid and sensitive in character than I already was by disposition and habit. This tendency was in reality at work; and I have little doubt that the effect in after-life would have been prejudicial, had not a new source of interest been supplied, and a new object presented itself for the exercise of my affections, which was to make me feel once more that I had a place in society, and an object in life.

CHAPTER III.

ALICE BRUCE.

"A creature not too bright or good
For human nature's daily food;
For transient sorrows, simple wiles,
Praise, blame, love, kisses, tears, and smiles."

WORDSWORTH.

MY fifteenth birthday was ushered in by the arrival of my aunt Alice, another widowed sister of my mother.

The loss of an only and beloved daughter, who, together with one son, alone, out of a family of six, had survived the period of infancy, coupled with some decrease in her funds, had induced my aunt to abandon a home now left desolate by the death of one of her children and the absence of the other, to take up her residence with her sister Dorothea.

Her coming was the advent of joy to me, and of some degree of relief to her own wounded spirit.

When the first bustle of her arrival had

passed over, and greetings and welcomes had been given, warmly on my part, and with something less than her usual frigidity on the part of her sister, and received by my poor aunt Alice with a flutter of feeling between smiles and tears, there was a dead pause.

And now came back the thoughts which the preparations for her journey, and that journey itself, had for a time diverted. It is in a moment like this that we feel most acutely what we have lost. While the mind is roused to the necessity of exertion, the pervading feeling of desolation is kept in abeyance. But this point once passed the heart sinks back upon itself; and memories of the past, and aching anticipations of the future, are all that fill up the dreary blank of life.

The first few days passed over unmarked by anything beyond vain efforts on the one hand to resist depression, and on the other to relieve it. Dorothea, with her usual blindness, continued to probe the wound instead of healing it; and as her poor sister's tears flowed afresh with every pang thus unnecessarily inflicted, an expression of satisfaction would steal over her rigid features; till, finding that the power of torture could go no further, she would rise from her seat with a self-possessed, self-approving air of magisterial importance, and sailing out of the room, leave the exhausted sufferer to "deal with grief alone."

Excluded from all sympathy where it should have been most abounding, the mourner, ever gentle and uncomplaining, instead of resenting a coldness which nevertheless she felt acutely, only turned with a more relying tenderness to the bosom ever ready to give sigh for sigh, and tear for tear. And now as time went on, beautiful was the affection which sprung up between us—between the motherless child and the childless mother.

I call her childless, for unchilded she was in a double sense, although her son yet remained to her; since by one of those unaccountable turns and shifts in the strange machinery of fate, this child, at the very thought of whom her whole soul overflowed with tenderness, had been torn from her.

Her husband, some time previous to the boy's birth, had exhibited unequivocal signs of insanity. His family termed these occasional aberrations, "eccentricity of manner;" some hesitated not to attribute them to hereditary disease; while others, with more reason, supposed his derangement to arise from local injury, the result of a severe attack of brain fever, from which he had never wholly recovered.

As these symptoms increased in strength and frequency, the maniac—for such in reality he was—began to evince an intolerable aversion to his unoffending wife. This at first showed itself merely in avoidance of her society, and in studied and determined opposition to her observance of the forms of the Roman Catholic faith which she professed; for he, like my aunt Dorothea, was a rigid Sectarian. No sooner, however, was his son born, than, seizing the opportunity to deal a cruel and deadly blow, he immediately made over the boy to the care of his own family; and, with the cunning natural to the insane, set about making a will, by which the mother was to be debarred from the presence or knowledge of her child until he should come of age. The reason he alleged—for he was still plausible enough to secure to himself all the privileges of a person of sound mind—was, that women were, from want of capacity, unfit to have the guardianship of male children.

Soon after this he died, utterly and hopelessly deranged. But the time of appeal was past.

His family, tenaciously alive to the taint of

insanity resting upon their name, which it would have done had the validity of the document been called in question, acted up, in every point, to the instructions contained in it. And as the bereaved mother, the only person whose interest it was to contest the will, refrained from doing so, the wrong, as usual, prevailed, and injustice triumphed.

These circumstances she herself communicated to me during those happy days—happy at least to me—which we passed together. Now would her eyes overflow with all a mother's tenderness, while depicting, with the eloquence of affection, the beauty and the virtues of her buried child; and now would she trace in imagination the features of that which still survived, but whose very form was a sealed book to her. In such moments she would delight to picture him rich in every grace of person, and in all those intellectual endowments which make the nobility of mind.

Sharing in such anticipations, and sympathising in such emotions, I was by degrees insensibly led to the contemplation of ideal perfections. The power was already at work, secretly and silently, which was to transform the unruffled heart of childhood into the troubled wellspring of woman's abounding affections—abounding to destruction and desolating unto death!

The aspects of the outer world, too, here lent their insidious aid to the accomplishment of that hidden transformation which was daily going on.

The house we inhabited was situated on the coast, immediately behind a range of chalk cliffs. Leading from it was a narrow winding road, verging downwards towards the water's edge, and presenting at its base an abrupt opening to the sea, formed by a division or chasm in the rocks. This little inlet, in connection with the natural excavations which were numerous in its neighbourhood, had given to the spot the name of Cavern Bay.

Here, while the stealing ocean rippled softly over the smooth level sand, or broke in ruder surges against the giant cliffs, the mind was alternately soothed and raised by the contemplation of nature in its aspects of placid loveliness or profound sublimity.

Nor were the warmer tints of woods and fields wanting to relieve the eye from the grander beauties of coast scenery. The same range of barren, chalky heights, which here formed a natural bulwark against the encroachments of the sea, terminated, farther on, in a sloping and slightly-wooded point, called "Rock's End." Here bloomed the sea-convolvulus, and waved the wild fennel. Here, too, the yellow-hammer and the linnet, nested safely in the very lap of the great deep, mingled their songs with the plaintive note of some solitary gull, which, uttering for a moment its lonely cry overhead, took its way far out to sea. Here, also, might be seen the night-heron, stalking in the moonlight along the edge of the bog-rushes which grew just above high-water mark, and seeking its prey among the shallows. Farther inland, the lark would spring up suddenly from the green corn, startling the ear with its melodious trill, amid the more than silence of the ocean murmur, and telling of man and man's labours amid scenes which spoke only of God.

Here day by day I wandered in a world of my own creation; a world in which there was no guile; a world which has now become resolved into its elements again.

And yet, not all. Some things remain— memories which are the sepulchres of what has been; the "graves of a household" spread far and wide.

As some lone cemetery, with its dull cypresses and tombstones, greets the traveller of the eastern wild, serving but to show that the waste has once been inhabited ; so, in looking back, the world of our young creation lies stretched out before us ; but for its dwellers—the sirocco has swept over them, and their place is no more!

CHAPTER IV.

THE ANNOUNCEMENT.

> " Heaven, receive
> A mother's thanks—a mother's tears of joy."
> BYRON.

THE time was now fast approaching which was to restore the son to his parent, the mother to her child. Who shall picture the overflowing feeling of delight that filled the heart of Alice Bruce, as the hour drew near which was to restore to her the child she longed to fold to her bosom, but whose face she had never beheld since its first infancy!

It was now late in the month of May, and in the following June would be summed up one and twenty years since she had brought him into life, and nursed him in joy upon her breast.

As the days wore on, she became restless and uneasy starting at every casual sound, and listening with an intensity of eagerness to every step that approached the house.

At last the long-looked-for announcement came. A letter was one morning placed before her, the writing of which she instantly recognised as that of her husband's brother. The seal, too, bore the well-remembered saltire of the ancient coat of Brus.

Her hand trembled as she received it; and a moment elapsed before she could summon courage to peruse the contents. It was couched in the coldest and most distant terms, merely intimating the arrival of her son from the Continent, where he had passed the last three years in company with a fellow-student; and proceeding to say, that on the 20th of June, his birthday, he would quit the residence of his uncle, where he was then staying, to pay his duty to his mother.

And was this all? No word from him—not a line? Was he so strict in his duty to his dead parent that he had no consideration for the living? Would he adhere to the very letter of his father's ban, and give no token of his existence to her who loved him best on earth, until the very last hour of her sacrifice should be worked out; not even now when he was free to follow the bent of his own feelings? This was bitter. Yet she bore it; blaming only those who might be supposed to have the guardianship of his 'actions, but casting no shadow of reproach on him.

But though this day she was troubled, and continued to wander restlessly from room to room, in the vain effort to find rest—somewhere, anywhere—from the tumult of her thoughts, the morrow brought healing on its wings: another letter came, bearing the same postmark, but in a different hand.

What could this mean? In a moment she was filled with a thousand apprehensions. Had anything happened to him; and was this indeed the death-blow to all her hopes, when on the very eve of their fulfilment?

It was strange that, although on the previous day she had wondered that her son had not written, the idea that he had done so never struck her now. She sank back in her chair, pale as death, pointing to the letter which she had not power to open. I immediately broke the seal, and turning to the signature, at once imparted the welcome intelligence that it was indeed from Francis himself.

Scarcely could I persuade her that this was not a deception. Again and again did she pore over the beloved characters, half blinded by her tears. Again and again did she press the name to her lips, reading and re-reading the precious scroll over and over till every word was perfect in her heart.

It was, indeed, a letter calculated to send joy to a mother's breast—so full of youth's warmest and freshest feelings—so sensible—so tender! The cause of his previous silence, Francis here explained; but hurriedly, and evidently in strong excitement under the influence of the new interests opened to him, and the glad affections from which he had been so long shut out. It was evident that he had been deceived as to his mother's real position and character, though, I was glad to find, in a way that saved his uncle from the imputation of wilful wrong. But all further explanations were reserved for the meeting. On that, and that alone, did he dwell with the fervour of anticipation, which, in youth's abounding season of the heart, doubles the enjoyment of every accorded blessing.

And in the midst of this joy, where was Dorothea? Encased in that armour of proof wherewith she had fenced her soul, she was invulnerable to every heartfelt emotion. Not a tear did she shed; not a pulse was quickened. She exhorted her sister to prayer, to thanksgiving. So far, this was well; for prayer can never be wrong, and thanks are always due. But she did not rest here. She blamed her in the harshest terms, and pointed out the sinfulness of allowing herself to be absorbed in worldly emotions.

Dear God! were not the uplifting of the mother's eye, and the sudden clasping together of the hands; the accents of blessing poured out upon the child so newly found; the tears of joy; the sighs of the overburthened heart; were not these the very spirit of thanksgiving? Were not these the very soul of prayer?

Oh! none are so mistaken as the unhumanised. None are so awfully misled as those who would seal up the fountains which God has given to flow. To check the love which purifies the intercourse with our kind on earth; to stifle the joy which softens the soul, and prepares it for heaven; to kneel down and call upon our Maker to witness and approve the deliberate annihilating, the taking away of the very *life* of that being with which He has endowed us; if there is an unseen, unuttered blasphemy of heart, it is this.

But, thanks to the trust that is within us, such counsels avail little. No sooner were we alone than we threw the feelings, thus for a time suppressed, into one long embrace. We mingled once more the tears of love and thankfulness; and praised God silently, and in the fulness of our hearts.

Week after week crawled on with sluggish pace; day followed day, and hour succeeded hour. At length the morning dawned that would lead us on to the eve of that day which was to be watched for with unsleeping eyes.

There was a more than ordinary bustle in the little household. The servants moved about more briskly than they were wont, and seemed to have caught the infection of pleasurable anticipation. The piano was, for a wonder, unopened; but a song of home was placed uppermost upon the volumes of music which occupied the cabinet beneath, and which, for the first time, had been unremoved for the morning's practice. Flowers were arranged in every vase with a more than usually careful hand. There was a little chamber above, commanding a view of the sea, which had been set apart for my cousin. This was now fitted up with everything that could possibly add to the comfort of its future inhabitant; and every article of furniture arranged and re-arranged by hands that trembled in their eagerness. The window was too deeply curtained; it made the room look gloomy. This was altered. Then it was too light; the rays of the sun entered too piercingly. A slighter muslin was now hung up in graceful folds, shadowing a little of the light, but not too much. A jar of flowers, was placed on the toilette-table, another on the drawers; to be removed, however, at night, out of considerations of health. Then there was a small table wheeled to one side, with blotting-book, pens, ink, and paper. But the one most notable arrangement by the mother's hand, was the careful suspending from the wall, immediately over the little *prie-dieu*, of a choice crucifix, a cross of ebony on which was imaged in ivory the crucified Saviour. In short, long before all was completed, although the mind kept up the body wonderfully, the limbs began to tire, for my aunt was not strong; and at last, all being finished, we sat down to contemplate our work.

We were disturbed out of a reverie into which we had both fallen, by the entrance of Dorothea, bearing in her hands a Bible and prayer-book. These were presented to her sister, and respectfully and gratefully accepted; and as no remark was made about such sacred deposits having been already supplied, Dorothea looked somewhat surprised when, on turning to place them upon the table, she found her intentions forestalled. There lay, not ostentatiously exposed to view, but sufficiently near at hand, the volumes which had often and often imparted peace to the suffering and widowed heart of my poor aunt Alice. There reposed the "Roman Breviary," "The Lives of the Saints," together with Heigham's "Exposition of the Holy Mass," and other devout works, the enlightened companions and solacers of the Christian soul.

Now this slight act on the part of Dorothea was in itself both kind and laudable. But it was the manner of doing it, or rather the spirit in which it was done, that took from it all the grace and beauty of kindness.

For the first time for many a day, Dorothea smiled as she turned towards her widowed sister. But somehow the smile was not genuine—not heart-warm. There was something sinister in it; a shade of—what shall I say—malignity? That is a harsh word. Yet I can find no other which at all conveys my meaning. The grave rebuke which was meant to be indicated by her offering, was here turned against herself. Had she supposed that a mother, of all others, was likely to forget, in ministering to the needs of the mortal creature, the safety and welfare of the immortal soul? Was that smile a cover for the shame she felt; shame for having made the hallowed tokens she held in her hand the medium of a mean and underhand rebuke? Or were other and less amiable feelings called forth in that unsympathising breast by the sight of those symbols of a more ancient faith spread out before her? Certain it is that the momentary visiting of compunction, if such it were, did not last long. Her eye glanced towards the wall where the crucifix had been hung. *That*, to her soulless and unimaginative nature, was an offence too great. She gave no second look, but retreated hastily from the room.

That night there were eyes that closed not till it was almost dawn. But when they did, sweet were the dreams that fell upon their shut lids. She who was to me a friend and a mother, and whose arms were clasped about me—for we shared the same bed—dropped her quiet head upon my breast, and breathed softly in her sleep. And for me, the light-winged cares that had buzzed and fretted round me during the day, were caught up and hushed in the bosom of sleep, like insects prisoned in the closing flower! That day's sun had gone down in peace; and the night became filled with forms that chased away its darkness. The peopled slumbers of the happy are filled with visions of an earthly paradise; but the dream of the pure in heart is heaven itself.

CHAPTER V.

THE ARRIVAL.

"What awful joy !——
Is it that feeble Nature calls her back,
And breaks her spirit into grief again?
                    Dearly pays the soul
For lodging ill."
                            YOUNG.

THE morning of the 20th of June was heralded in with the songs of birds twittering on every bough, and giving promise of a brilliant summer day. The blackbird might be seen running swiftly through the dewy grass, or lighting on a low bough to plume his wings for more lengthy flights. The chaffinch and the cunning jay were already abroad, seeking their early repast. The night-wind had sighed itself to rest, and the sea sent scarcely the sound of a single ripple up to our sheltered haven. Hearts that had sunk down to slumber, weary with hope, were aroused in gladness; and eyes which had woke up somewhat dim from their overnight's vigil, now looked forth and received the impress of the brightness and beauty from without.

We were that morning more subdued and silent than usual. But there was at times a slight hurriedness of manner, and a quickness to oblige each other, which told that our hearts were full, and softened and harmonised by the happiness within.

I speak, of course, only of my aunt Alice and myself; for Dorothea spent her mornings alone; and, indeed, at all other times was so wrapt within herself, and kept up so cold a seclusion from the little world around her, that she had necessarily no sympathies in common with us.

I have said that my aunt Alice was not strong. She was one whose feelings were not loud but deep. The miseries she endured silently, and without complaint, during the two years previous to her widowhood, followed by the bitterest trial of all—the loss of her daughter, had shaken her constitution materially. This was occasionally evidenced by a sudden and unaccountable failure of bodily strength; by a depression of animal spirits, greater than the immediate occasion called for;

by frequent and apparently causeless fluctuations of colour, and by violent palpitations of the heart.

Towards the noon of the day in question, these last and more alarming indications were manifested to a greater degree than usual. She had risen in the morning without a vestige of colour in her face. In an hour or two she became flushed; and towards the middle of the day complained of violent spasms in the region of the heart.

Some slight restorative was administered; and as by degrees the alarming symptoms abated, and she declared herself free from pain, I felt reassured, and gradually dismissed all apprehension from my mind.

But not so did my aunt Alice. Whatever pain she suffered from that time, she kept it to herself. But a change had come over the tone of her feelings. An internal conviction had taken possession of her mind that her death was near at hand.

There was now in her manner an excitement foreign to it; an impatience of the slow progress of time; a constant reference to the hour. All this would, after a while, give place to the languor of exhaustion. And as she lay on the sofa, her head reclining gently backwards and her eyes closed, I felt comforted by the fallacious hope that she was resting and gathering strength.

But the fever of the mind is not so easily allayed where the exciting cause is "not dead, but sleepeth." She did not speak. She gave no token of what was passing within. But the thought was presenting itself—should she live to see him? Would this child of her love, unseen but cherished, return to her arms but to be welcomed by the cold embrace of death? Were they never to take sweet counsel together; and was the precious wellspring of affection never to be breathed on by the breath of joy, until its waters could no longer be stirred —until the ice had closed over all?

Evening was now drawing on; and with every hour expectation was deepened into painfulness. As the different vehicles passed and re-passed along the metropolitan road, every wheel in its approach towards the house sent the blood to that heart already filled to stifling.

At last the loose rattling sound of a chaise was heard. Nearer and nearer it rolled; it stopped. A youthful face was half visible in the twilight, looking eagerly out. There was a startling knock: a sudden springing of a light form down the steps. In another moment the parent would be in the arms of the child.

And what meanwhile was going on within? The mother's ear and eye were the first to awake to the joyful truth. In an instant she had rushed from the window to the door. There had scarcely been time for her to have reached the stairs, when we were startled by a faint cry, succeeded by a sudden and heavy fall.

I flew to her side. There, indeed, in the arms of the son lay the mother. But how? Rigid, and stiffening in a fit: her teeth ground together till the blood sprung out, and mingled with the foam that oozed upon her lips! Joy had done the work of grief. From that hour the days of Alice Bruce were numbered.

Medical assistance was promptly summoned. But little could be done; and we awaited the return to consciousness in fear and trembling. Silence and caution were advised, together with the avoidance of everything that could excite the patient on the first indication of restored sensibility.

This was most difficult. Should the faculties of the mind awake from their present torpor, memory would be busy to recall the causes of that excitement which had led to so painful a result.

The Arrival.

Her recovery was slow. Two hours elapsed before the sufferer could be pronounced out of immediate danger. As by little and little her thoughts began to collect themselves, and gather some indistinct knowledge of the change that had fallen upon us all—and most of all on her—it became, of course, impossible to keep silence upon the one most important point— the arrival of Francis.

It is true that she had no recollection of having seen him; although the cry we had heard had burst from her lips when first she saw him rush up the stairs to meet her. Yet to have told her that he had not arrived, would only have been to keep up her expectations, and increase her anxiety to a pitch of irritability which, under the circumstances, would have been most ill-advised.

Cautiously, therefore, I undertook the hazardous task of communicating to her the fact that her son had arrived; that he was actually in the house; but that the doctor had decidedly forbidden her seeing him until she should be sufficiently restored to bear an interview so trying to the feelings of both.

It was all in vain. She *must* see him; she was better; she *would* be calm. She dwelt upon all she had suffered for his sake, and thought us cruel in shutting her out from the sight of her child.

Finding all my attempts useless, and fearing the worst if I any longer denied this natural wish, I, with the doctor's consent, summoned Francis to the sick chamber.

She was right. Nature is ever our best guide. She saw him, wept over him, blessed him, and was calm.

And now, having prevailed upon her to part with him for awhile, she was left to my care alone; and pressing a kiss upon her forehead, and forbidding her to speak another word, I had soon the comfort of seeing her sink into a tranquil and profound sleep.

So ended that day, which rose so brightly, but which was destined to so dark a close; a day which had been looked for in the hopefulness of the heart, and welcomed in the confidence of the spirit. Could we have known by anticipation two months ago, what had now come to pass, how would our hope have been darkened, and our joy turned into mourning! Grateful is the veil which falls upon the things to come, and merciful the hand that drops it! By this are we enabled to walk on in smiles, and bless the guiding Power that lights us on our way. And if our path be dark, we know at least that, whether it leads us onward to the green spots of life or to the pitfalls of the world, that Guide is still faithful to us, and to the interests not of the Here but of the Hereafter ; and does all, and directs all, not with the flaming sword of terror and dismay, but secretly and silently, and in the spirit of love and chastening.

CHAPTER VI.

THE CLIFF.

" There is a cliff whose high and bending head
Looks fearfully in the confined deep.
                        How fearful
And dizzy 'tis to cast one's eyes so low !"
                        SHAKESPEARE.

IN preparing to retrace the portion of my history which now lies before me, I feel inclined to pause, and to consider whether it is likely that the power will indeed be given me to trace the gradual working out of those scenes and events which tended materially to change my character and alter my views of life both as to this world and the world to come. Often do I feel tempted to throw aside the task, and to exclaim, " What will it avail ?" Supposing even that I were enabled to recall, and fix for ever in unalterable hues, some part of the portraiture of a life whose interest consists more in its inward existence of thought and feeling, than in its mere outward accidents; still, much of what should be retained has necessarily passed into oblivion; much has undergone that change which the maturity of the mind effects upon the beings of the past, causing us to behold them with altered eyes, and to judge them at a different tribunal: still more is there, the understanding of which it is impossible to convey to others. The strongest feelings, the deepest passions, are those which never find a voice.

Still, with all this—the probable futility of unravelling for the benefit of others our own past experiences, and the inability we feel to do justice to so important a design—still the hope, however distant, of being useful to our kind, by opening the hidden source of tears, and drawing to light those bitter poisons which lie concealed within the honey-flowers of life, is a sufficient incitement to a labour for which the accomplishment of that hope would be a sufficient reward. It is enough if we are enabled to open the eyes of those who, like Harpastes, knowing not they are blind, desire to be led abroad, exclaiming, " The house is dark !"

It was some time before things got into their usual train. Eventually, my aunt was partially restored to health: that is, she was able to leave her bed; and, subsequently, her room. But it soon became evident to herself, although we were yet unconscious of the pang which awaited us, that nature was gradually sinking; and that, however she might rally for weeks, or even perhaps for months, the seal of death was no less assuredly set upon her brow.

And now all the beauty and the truth, the trust, the devotedness of her woman's nature were daily and hourly developed. Although life was becoming every moment more endeared to her, not a complaint, not a murmur was ever heard from her lips, that could indicate how sorely she felt the doom which was to shut her out from it for ever. She was yet in the matronly prime of her years; and much as she had undergone, her feelings had never been deadened or *unyouthed*. She had not to sink into the grave with the comforting thought that she was laying down a burthen greater than she could bear; she had to go down to darkness with the thrilling consciousness of an increased power of enjoyment strengthening within her. The passage to the grave, too, was to be trodden alone, without the sympathy which smooths the bed of the dying. None knew but herself what was going on within. She did not regret this; she rejoiced at it; but not the less did she feel it. She assumed a cheerfulness which was but a mask for the melancholy that devoured her. Like the poor Hindoo, while writhing in the pangs of her self-imposed penance, she scattered flowers around her. She smiled; but her smiles were but as sun-rays upon the tomb; they might gladden and chase the thoughts of corruption from those who were *without*—but she was *within* its shadow.

Her whole thoughts were now directed to the future prospects of her son. Fortune he would have none, beyond the little she could bequeath him at her death. His father had been a younger brother, and brought up to the Church. After passing his best years as a poor country curate, he eventually obtained a small living, barely sufficient for the maintenance of himself and family; and at his death his widow would have been left wholly unprovided for, but for the small patrimony which had been settled upon her at her marriage.

It is true, that the uncle with whom Francis had been reared, himself childless, had always declared his intention of making him his heir;

and, under this idea, had not educated him for any profession. But Sir Richard Bruce was a man of strong passions, haughty, and overbearing; and any offence, however unintentional on the part of his nephew, might at once place him beyond the pale of his uncle's favour.

At the best, therefore, the prospects of Francis were doubtful. And although he himself, youth-like, dwelt lightly on these points, he was yet not insensible to the dependence of his position, and would willingly have exchanged his more splendid, expectations for others less brilliant but unconditional upon personal caprice.

With his mother this was a source of much uneasiness. Yet she was not without hope that even in the event of the worst, his youth and natural abilities would still open to him the path of honourable exertion, and raise him to that station in society which he was every way fitted to assume.

During the months that intervened between that fatal 20th of June and the final closing of the scene, I had sufficient opportunity of observing every individual trait in the character of my cousin. Never, it seemed to me, was there a being more formed for goodness than was Francis. His manly tenderness towards his mother; his ever ready suggestion of some plan for the relief of the sufferer; his mirth that cheered; his very seriousness that gladdened the heart more than mirth; these were to me no less conspicuous in him than were his correct judgment; his frank ingenuousness; his abhorrence of vice, and his unbounded love of virtue.

Unsubdued by any misgivings as to the stroke that awaited me, and feelingly alive to every source of pleasure, both outwardly in the world of inanimate nature, and inwardly in the more sensitive world of my own breast, I now began, unconsciously, to indulge in that delicious intercourse of mind which makes a paradise of youth—or rather, which youth makes a paradise.

In this mysterious, this wonderful lighting up of the living landscape before us, it is not in the things themselves that the charm lies, but in that peculiar faculty whereby the soul transforms every object of sense into something divine. Unknown to myself, I was gradually lending wings to those imaginations which were destined to hover over and impart to every conceivable object colours not its own. Every leaf, every flower, was now to become glorified, and every familiar spot made sacred, by the presence of one whose memory in after years was to darken them with its shadow.

There is no moment in the life of woman which thrills her whole being with such conflicting emotions as that in which she first becomes conscious that she loves. The deep well of affection in her heart may have been sounded, and the innermost depths of her soul fathomed, by the power which is destined to abide with her through life, for good or for evil; and yet she herself may remain unconscious of the change that is wrought within her, until by some unforeseen accident, some awakening circumstance, slight perhaps in itself, the veil is all at once rent from her eyes, and she beholds and shudders at the abyss which lies stretched out before her.

Nearly a year had passed over our heads since our first meeting; and during the whole of that period, Francis and myself had scarcely spent a single day out of each other's society. The same duties, the same pleasures were ours. Ours was the task to support the drooping head, and raise the sinking spirit; to read to, and to watch over in a thousand nameless ways, the beloved sufferer who was to us both as a common mother. Or when, fearful of tasking us too far, she would towards evening insist on our leaving her, and taking a stroll upon the beach, what a joy it was to bend our steps, elastic with youth, down to the borders of that majestic ocean which seemed to image to our souls their own boundless capacities, and to awake within us thoughts too great for utterance, thoughts too extended for the narrow sphere of this world, too high for mortality, too full of heaven for the communion of earth!

On one of these occasions it was that, finding the sands left wet by the late ebbing of the tide, we had varied our path by taking that which led upwards towards the summit of the cliff, and which conducted to the wooded point already alluded to under the name of Rock's End.

We had reached that part of the cliff where it first loses somewhat of its perpendicular form, and where the barren whiteness of the chalk becomes relieved to the eye by the growth of a few stunted and straggling bushes, scattered at intervals, and firmly enough rooted in their shallow soil, or crevice-beds, amidst the fissures, or along narrow ledges of the rock.

We here paused to contemplate a group of

children who were playing within a few yards of the precipice; running here and there in a sort of mimic chase, in the full exuberance of animal spirits; and shouting to each other till the rocks rang to the echo of their voices. A little apart from her more giddy companions was a girl somewhat older than the rest, whose excursions were more confined by her having in her charge a healthy-looking little fellow, who was indulging in that peculiar species of locomotion common to very young children.

We remained thus watching their youthful gambols, until the chillness of the evening warned us to proceed, when we once more continued our walk towards the point.

We had not proceeded far, when suddenly an alarm was given by the group we had left; and a second and more piercing cry from the elder girl instantly suggested to us that some accident must have happened to the infant.

We lost no time in retracing our steps; and now the eager and dismayed faces of the children as they bent over the cliff in search of something below, directed our attention to the real nature of the evil.

The girl, it appeared, having heedlessly joined in the pursuit of the other children, had left the infant to itself, when the little creature must have tumbled and rolled itself over and over, until at last it reached the very verge of the cliff, and was at once precipitated from its summit.

Fortunately, as we soon ascertained, the child had been arrested in its fall midway by a straggling bush, and now hung suspended among the lighter branches, from which the least movement on its part threatened to precipitate it to the sands below, a distance of at least a hundred feet.

Before I could recover from the shock, or think what was to be done, Francis had thrown off his coat, so as to be unencumbered in his movements, and was preparing to descend the cliff.

I was aghast, unnerved by terror. What was he about to do? it was madness—it was almost certain death. I seized his arm and struggled to detain him. In my agony I could have knelt to him. Perhaps I did; I know not. The horror of his death—a death so fearful, and before my very eyes—rose up before me, and I knew not what I did or what I said. My whole soul rose to my lip. In vain I besought—in vain I prayed him by all he loved—by all who loved him, not to go. Alas! I might have spoken to the winds.

His only answer, while he pointed below, was, "Dora, can you see *that*, and yet wish me not to make the attempt?"

Before, I had not dared to look upon the child; now, I did not dare to look at Francis. There was in his eye something between astonishment and reproach, which abashed— which stung me. I dropped my eye beneath his glance—I loosed my hold. In another moment he was descending the cliff.

Cautiously, and with a steady foot, now resting on a projecting ledge of rock, and now balancing himself by catching hold of a stray branch, he proceeded upon his perilous mission, followed by the straining eyes of the anxious group above.

And other eyes were tracing his progress, step by step; but not as theirs did—not with the thrill of anxious hope, but in all the frozen calmness of a despair beyond the power of imagination to picture. I felt as if every step he advanced was my death-blow. I looked upon his destruction as certain, and awaited my doom with the rigidness and fixedness of a statue. My doom? why mine? God of Heaven; what had changed me from the being I had been, to the being I was? Why was that child's peril—its sister's agony, actual and present—its mother's wretchedness and desolation to come—its father's silent misery, why were these things to me as if they had not been? Was every touch of womanly pity, every feeling of common humanity, dead within me? What had wrought this change?

How he reached the spot I know not; but he did reach it. The rest was easy. Taking the little one in his arms, he continued his downward path, where, from the increased thickness of the bushes, the descent was now comparatively without danger. At last he reached the base, and proceeded in the direction of Rock's End, with the intention of rounding the point.

I should have flown to meet him. Why did I not? Did my limbs refuse their office? No: terror had, indeed, unnerved me; but it was something different from this which kept me rooted to the spot. What had I said?—what had I done? What feelings had I betrayed, not to myself only, but to him? How could I meet him now? Oh! at that moment how gladly could I have sprung from the dizzy height on which I stood, down to the gulf that yawned beneath me!

As he approached nearer and nearer, I longed for the earth to cover me. He appeared excited by the scene; and spoke much, and with animation. This was a relief. And now, having consigned the child to the eager and grateful hands stretched out to receive it, we took our way homewards.

My head was still in a whirl, and I made this an excuse for retiring at once to my room. No sooner was I alone than I gave vent to those tears of agony which can flow but once in a lifetime. They did not soothe me: but I could not stop them. The fountain of anguish seemed never to be dried up. Until this day I had been a child, and had wept the tears of a child. This was the woman's first agony—and it was a deadly one.

CHAPTER VII.

THE DEATH-BED.

"When Faith and Love, which parted from thee never,
Had ripen'd thy just soul to dwell with God,
Meekly thou didst resign this earthly load
Of death, called life."
                          MILTON.

"Death, be not proud, though some have called thee
Mighty and dreadful, for thou art not so."
                          DONNE.

IT may possibly be thought that the feelings here portrayed as called into action by the scene described, are overwrought; that they are essentially unnatural, and more than the occasion called for. Were our world a world of realities only, I grant this might be so. But we are the creatures of imagination, no less than the slaves of conscience.

In vain did I represent to myself that the interest I had felt and expressed for Francis was no more than was warranted by the relation in which we stood to each other. If this were so, what meant the look of astonishment which had so abashed me? Could this be fancy?—No, I felt that it was too real. In an unguarded moment I had yielded to the innate selfishness of my nature. The agony of terror which overmastered me on his account had betrayed me into a forgetfulness of the humanity due to others; and it was for *him* to teach me the lesson of mercy. The reproach conveyed by his words—oh, how it sunk into my soul! I felt lost, utterly lost; degraded in my own eyes, and despicable in the eyes of him whom I loved with all the energy of a quick and devoted spirit. Yes, loved—and without a return of love! I could no longer conceal from myself that it was so. I had tasted of the bitter fruits of knowledge, and could no more return to my first Eden.

Still, in spite of the momentary weakness into which I had been surprised, I knew the resources of my own mind too well to doubt my power of self-control when I should have time to think and to act. From the moment that my resolution was taken, and my rule of action laid down, I felt happier and more at ease. Now was the time to prove the meanness or the nobleness of the passion with which my whole being was informed. I knew its purity, and I had faith in its strength. I felt no shame in that love itself: it is the colour which our best feelings assume in the eyes of others that reflects back the blush to our own cheek.

But let me do what I would, strive as I might, the beauty of life had faded from me. The joyous and unrestrained intercourse in which I had till now indulged, was at an end. The freshness of existence had departed; the youth of my heart was gone for ever.

A night passed in tears was not the best preparation for a day of struggles. The dreaded hour of rising came; and, though firm in every good resolve, I felt weakened and agitated. And now I had to meet him, and to put on a mask for the first time in my life.

Had he greeted me coldly, or shown the least token of retaining any unpleasant remembrance of what had occurred, I think I could have borne it without the slightest betrayal of my feelings: my pride would have been roused. But how different was his manner! He took my hand in his with a kindlier pressure than usual. His voice was more than ever tender in its tone. He was pale, too; yet I thought he coloured slightly; and he looked jaded, as if he had not slept.

As my eyes met his, I felt the tears rising, and turned away. For an instant—it was *but* an instant—the thought presented itself, 'Could it be, was it possible, that the self-same accident had withdrawn the shield from *both* our hearts?"

Fortunately for me, in one sense, although the cause was a trying one, my thoughts and feelings were soon to be directed into another channel. My aunt was rapidly growing worse. Her life, like a half-shed flower, was dropping its leaves one by one. As I saw her dying daily before my eyes, I could not meet her patient smile, her look of love, her fond embrace, and retain one thought of self. Not for worlds would I have cast upon that gentle breast the burthen which oppressed my own. The gloom of the grave was deepening round me, and all other griefs were lost in its shadow.

As the dreaded hour of her departure drew near, the approach of death seemed to silence the stirrings of life and life's passions in my heart. It was as if my soul were gathering up its forces against the hour of strife; the hour when I should be left to battle with the world alone. Alone!—oh, the pains, the stings, the weariness, that are compassed in that little word! We may say what we will of the emptiness of life—every-day, social life; but let those who know not what real solitude is—try it! Let them wear out the day, and day after day, in the dull, heavy, grave-like hush of the entranced; feelingly alive, but dead to all the uses of humanity. Let them linger out an existence which has not even the privilege of vegetation—community of soil. Let them rise with a sigh whose very echo shall startle them in the silent chamber of their unrest; and let them sink down on their bed at night, spirit-haunted. People may talk lightly of the present: those whose tide of life is full of the kindly ebb and flow of home affections, may despise it if they will—unwisely. But the solitary has no present. It is not the impalpable medium, the blank atmosphere that surrounds him, of which he is sensible. It is the winds afar off, the Past and the Future, the rushing of whose wings *he* hears.

I will not dwell upon the scene which followed. Who that has ever visited the chamber of death, even a stranger's, can forget it?—who that has ever filled with their sobbing that of one beloved, would willingly recall it?

It is easy to picture the first. The silence, and the darkened room; the stealing steps; the heads bowed down; the voices tuned to woe;

the eyes' sleepless watch ; the hands' trembling ministry ; the curtained bed, from which comes upon the ear the stifled breathing of a creature about to die ; the pause in the respiration—that awful lull of the death-breeze ; the suddenly returning sob ; the faint dying away of the breath ; one gurgle ;—then a sigh—and all is over :—these are truths that come home to the bosoms of all.

But the death-bed of one we love ! All have not known this. There are some to whom this twofold wrenching out of the spirit of life is a mystery still. And who but those who have known it, can conceive it ? The desolate survivors—the left on earth, who shall portray them ? With them that silence is the dying away of their own heart. With them that darkened room is the yawning of their own grave. Every cautious step they take is one nearer to despair. Every tone of their voice is the death-wail of a parting hope. The watchfulness of their eyes, the ministering of their hands—these are the acts of the sleep-walker ; acts done in the body, but of which the mind has no consciousness. The limbs move about, here and there, wherever the little dream of this world's necessities impels them. But the soul is in that bed ; in the bed of the dying.

The Death-Bed.

The spirit is parted from its clay, as that spirit is parting. The sigh which goes forth from that poor worn-out husk, has in it no pang like the sigh which is echoed back from the vigorous and full of life! The sob of the dying is the exultation of a soul released. The writhing of the limb is but the spurning of the clay by the foot of the angel already winged for the skies. But the sob of the living—oh! that is the groan of the condemned. The shrinking, shuddering agony of the forsaken soul—oh! that is the casting down of both worshipper and idol; the doom of all things; the annihilation of earth and heaven!

The prayer of many a heart-sick year was answered. The eyes of the mother were closed by the hand of the child. The steps she had been forbidden to train, followed her to the grave; and the love she had yearned for, was poured out aboundingly upon her dust. The world might wreak its spite upon her now; she was beyond its malice. The tender relation of parent and child had been disturbed; but was no more distorted. The decrees of nature seemed not annulled, but reversed. The beauty of *his* childhood she had not seen; but the loveliness of *her* youth was present to him. The grace—the softness—

the placid, pure, angelic transcript of what she had been, rested visibly upon her brow, and chased away the crushing thought of what she was. The breath of this changeful world no sooner left her lip, than the evidence of the Changeless was there. It stole over her features—we knew not how. The trace of pain, the marks of suffering wore away—mysteriously, invisibly; and in their place there came—magically, and at once, the impress of peace; the calm of perfect rest; the smile of the accepted; the crowning glory of the ransomed, on which the Mighty had set His seal.

CHAPTER VIII.

A COMMUNICATION.

"Methinks I should not thus be led along
Mailed up in shame.
The earth has not a hole to hide this deed."
SHAKESPEARE.

IT is strange with what a light touch nature will sometimes knock at our breast, and sound the hollowness of all within. Autumn had advanced unperceived, and winter had set in. The last time I had looked abroad with eyes undimmed by inward grief, the outer world had worn all the beauty and the greenness of life. Now I looked forth—and not a leaf was on the trees!

And what a change had fallen upon our little household! How we missed the face so familiar to us! how we yearned for the sweet voice that was gone! How often, as the door opened, did we look suddenly up; forgetting, for the moment, that the eye we turned to meet was to smile on us no more!

Days, weeks, months, passed away; but our sorrow passed not away. We had lost, both I and Francis, the friend and the mother whose place no other could supply to us. The link was broken which no power could ever again unite. In as far as this affection had filled our hearts, they were henceforth to be void. We were no longer what we were. We thought it was the aspect of things without that was altered. Alas! it was in ourselves and in our own minds that the change lay.

It is with the youth of human beings as with the immature plant; one support gone, another must be sought. If the staff which upheld it be taken away, another must be supplied, or the plant will seek it for itself. If it finds the needful support, the scion may still thrive: if it finds it not, it perishes.

Desolate as our hearts were, and warm as were our affections, is it to be wondered at that we two—my cousin and myself—should have leaned towards each other for succour when the storm fell heaviest upon us? The agitating emotions which had contended in my breast had been partly laid at rest. The trying scene we had gone through together had chased from me for a time every feeling but the innocent and confiding tenderness of the sister for the brother. But the impressions I had received were too deep to be wholly erased. As time wore on, and everything settled down again into its accustomed course, my reserve returned, increased; and the same rigid self-inspection was maintained as before.

But the task was becoming a most difficult one. An alteration had taken place in Francis's manner towards me, for which I could not account. There was in it at times a restraint which almost chilled, but more frequently a warmth which startled me. The idea which most readily suggested itself I did not dare to indulge. That he loved me was too blest a belief: that he pitied me was death to think of. That he should have read my inmost heart, and discovered there a predilection authorised by no word or token on his part; and that he should have bestowed in return, not his love, but his compassion—the thought was too humiliating.

Why then did he remain with us? I was aware that he had frequently received letters from his uncle urging his return; and from the care with which he concealed from me the exact knowledge of their contents, I divined their purport in part. I knew that his family considered themselves above, and therefore debased by any communion with mine. But I did not yet know *all.* That blow was yet in reserve for me.

The grave had for many months been closed upon all we held dear, when, one morning, Dorothea, in a somewhat mysterious manner, summoned me to attend her in her room. It was with no little trepidation that I entered her presence; not knowing what I was about to encounter, and dreading the worst. Could it be that she, too, had read my heart? Or had Francis—but no, it could not be *that.* I scarcely knew why, but my heart died within me as she signed to me to close the door, and to seat myself by her side.

She was busied with some letters and papers which lay open on the table before her, and did not immediately address me. I had thus time to summon to my aid all the strength of mind I possessed, in order to bear as best I might the blow that awaited me.

When I recall the state of feeling in which I passed those few brief moments, I cannot help supposing that there must be some faculty of the human mind which is not known, and perhaps never will be known to us. That undefined, but no less certain indication of some overwhelming calamity about to happen to ourselves or to those near to us—how does it arise? whence does it come?

There was in the summons I received nothing which should have suggested any more serious communication than some mere matter of business; for my aunt's manner was always mysteriously impressive, even about trifles. Yet—how it was I know not—from the instant she desired me to attend her I felt that the very soul of life was departing from me. I could no more comprehend why I felt this, than I could divine the nature of the stroke about to fall; but I did feel it. I summoned up my courage to meet this unknown dispensation, whatever it might be. I cast from me every weakness, every tremor, as the martyr disrobes himself for the block. It seemed a thing against which there was no appeal.

At length she spoke. "Dora," she began, "you are now eighteen. By the blessing of Divine Providence you have till now been kept comparatively in wholesome ignorance of the crimes and backslidings of this evil world. You are, I hope and trust, fully aware of its iniquities generally; but they have not yet come home to you. The communication

I am about to make, I make according to the dying request of your departed mother. Have you sufficient resignation to the dispensations from above to bear whatever I may be about to tell you?"

I answered calmly, that I hoped I had. She then resumed—but why repeat in her own words what was cutting enough in itself, without the addition of her cold, unsympathising manner of imparting it?

The sum of what she told me was this. My father was in reality living, though I had always been led to believe that he died during my infancy.

He had, when a young man, entered into a mercantile house. While there, although barely earning a subsistence for himself, he had had the imprudence to marry. The increasing demands of a wife and child soon becoming more than he had funds to meet, he entered into various speculations one after another, each of which in its turn failed.

It is difficult to trace how, in a soil originally good, the seeds of dishonesty are sown, and the after-harvest of sin and shame, with all their accompanying load of horrors, entailed. Pressed by innumerable difficulties from without, and harassed in his home by the aspect of poverty and the daily sight of his wretched but ever gentle and uncomplaining wife, in an evil hour the tempter assailed him—and he fell. He forged a bill of exchange; was detected, prosecuted, convicted of felony, and condemned to suffer the extreme penalty of the law. Subsequently a reprieve was granted; and finally the sentence was commuted to transportation for life.

Here then were accounted for the suffering and the tears, the heartache and broken spirit of my poor lost mother.

She outlived this trial, bitter as it was. As a wife she would have sunk under it; but as a mother she bore all things for the sake of her child. She took leave tenderly of him who, in spite of everything, was her husband still and the father of her babe, and who, sinning and disgraced as he was, had yet erred and incurred shame for her; and in that interview bade farewell to him for ever.

Happily for the little rest that was left to her on earth, she did not survive to experience the torturing agony—the fear—the suspense —the dread—that was doomed to be the inheritance of her child. The time was shortly to come when, as I drained to the last drop the bitter cup presented to my lips,

I should thank my God that I suffered alone, and that she was "safe in the grave."

And now for the first time I learnt to whom my mother had been indebted for those comforts, and that security from the stings of poverty, which had happily fallen to her lot when her heart was the sorest. This was the work of my good aunt Alice!

For years my mother had received sum after sum from an unknown hand; and it was only when accident revealed to her in the name of the giver, that of a sister almost as poor as herself, that she was enabled to return all she had to return—the thanks of a grateful heart.

Such was the charity, "twice blessed," with which the bosom of that generous creature was filled even to overflowing. Many must have been the deprivations she suffered while ministering, in silence and secrecy, to the wants of her sister. This was, indeed, the "casting of the bread upon the waters;" and in the love which I bore her, and which blessed her to the last, it may truly be said that "she found it after many days."

CHAPTER IX.

THE AVOWAL.

> "That comfort comes too late.
> 'Tis like a pardon after execution:
> That gentle physic given in time had cured me;
> But now I am past all comfort here, but prayers."
> SHAKESPEARE.

WHEN this Pandora's box of evil things—in which was not even a hope—had been poured out to the end, and Dorothea, perfectly satisfied in her own mind that I was as insensible to it all as she could wish, dismissed me from her presence, I found myself in my room, and alone.

The first thing that struck, and somewhat shocked me, was, that I felt so little emotion. I remember only that I felt oppressed. A kind of waking nightmare was upon me. A load had settled upon my breast, which I could not shake off. But there were no tears, no sighing.

The window was open. I walked up to it.

I looked out. There was the sun as ever shining broad and bright, and dazzling the eye with its reflection from the snow that lay deep on the ground.

I turned away. I sat down. My temples ached, and mechanically I raised my hand to my head. There was an involuntary movement;—my hand stole over my eyes, and pressed down their lids.

And now the thing in all its deformity rose up before me. But not at once. It developed itself slowly; piece by piece—limb by limb; till at last—there it stood, ghastly and hideous before me.

A convicted felon! Had I heard aright? The tender reverence in a child's heart, that breathes out in the name of "father!" where was it?

The thought made me pause. An impious suggestion rose within me. What had I done? how had I sinned, that these coals of fire should be heaped upon my head?

Whatever was to come; whether my days were to be "few and evil," or whether they were to be lengthened out into an eternity of misery—in the leprosy of shame and disgrace, *this* was an abiding wrong. It ended not with life. It was my birthright—my bitter inheritance, and must descend to all time. I could not hide it in the grave. The voice of outraged society; the cry of public derision;—these would drag it from darkness—these would startle it into life; and hatred, and scorn, and the world's malice, like bloodless vampires, would gloat and gorge upon it till their veins were full.

As the dreadful truth glared upon me I groaned in the bitterness of my soul. Pain and grief I had known already: already had my heart been rudely startled from its first dream of blessedness and peace: but I had known no sorrow which could be compared to this. It was not the breaking of one tie; it was the crushing of a whole existence. The brand was on my brow. Go where I would, I must bear it with me—the child of a *felon!*

There was one—and but one—source of congratulation still left to me. Dearly as I loved Francis—and *how* I loved him I had yet to prove—I could now rejoice that his fate was not involved in mine. I could now part with him calmly—gladly. I could hide myself from him and from the world; and whether I lived or died—and life and death were now equally indifferent to me—I should, at least, be spared the added pang of having brought sorrow and lasting infamy upon his beloved head.

But even this comfort was not to last me long. I thought fate had done its worst. Alas! the bitterest trial of all was yet to come.

It was long before my eyes were opened to the truth. But they were opened at last; and I saw that Francis loved me.

Ever since the hour that had first revealed to me the blot of infamy which rested on my name, I had withdrawn as much as possible from the intercourse with my cousin. I could not do this entirely; but I did what I could. I no longer passed my whole mornings with him, as I had used to do; walking out with him when the weather permitted, and at other times working while he read to me. Whenever it was possible, I stole away, and left him to himself, and wept secret and bitter tears in the desolation of my heart.

But I was tasking my soul beyond its strength. My health gave way; my spirits failed. They sunk woefully—utterly; and he saw it. And soon, by many a slight action, unobserved by all others, but unconsciously treasured up by me;—by many a word, tender as the thought it breathed;—by many a look which found its thrilling answer in my soul, I knew that I was beloved.

One little year back, what a joy would this have been! Joy! oh, what a feeble word is that! To know ourselves beloved where we have given our whole soul—irrevocably, and for ever—there is no heaven like it on this side the grave!

Never till then had I known the strength and the fervour, the devotedness and the self-sacrifice of the love I bore him. My tears were now shed for him, not for myself. Willingly—gladly, would I have died to give him peace. But what could I do? Were he to own his love to me, should I tell him the dreadful secret which had stung me to the heart, and throw myself upon his love and truth? Should I, to still the pain of the present, inflict misery upon him through all the long future?

I saw too plainly what would ensue. By an union with one beneath him in birth, and stained with a parent's shame, he would lose for ever the countenance of his uncle, the only living relative on whom he could rely for the means of subsistence. And would he not, as the years drew on, cramped by poverty, and lowered in the eyes of the world—would he not, secretly and, in his soul, if not openly, accuse me as the author of all; as the heartless, selfish being who, for her own love's sake, forgot the nobler purposes for which that love was given to her? I thought of all this, and I was strong.

But how deep was the struggle in my soul! That night, when, in the shadowy twilight of our little room—our affections softened into sadness, and our hearts melted and trembling to the influence of that holy hour—he spoke to me of love, what was the power that withheld me as I longed to throw myself upon his neck and sob out the tender joy that filled my whole being? Oh! what but the mournful consciousness of my woman's lot?—what but the deep, unutterable spirit of self-sacrifice? Something higher than joy, and mightier than despair!

He spoke in doubt; for he saw the struggle within me, incomprehensible as it seemed to him. He spoke in sorrow; for he felt that there was no hope. But earnestly, and passionately, and with all the energy of a nature as much above the weakness of woman as it was above the selfishness of man, did he pour out to me the fulness of his noble, but misplaced affection.

I listened. I drank with eager ear every tone of that beloved voice; and my heart stood still.

I did not withdraw my hand from the tender pressure of his; for that hand had been clasped there beside the death-bed of his parent, and the tears were scarcely yet dry which had been showered upon it then. I did not turn away from his gaze, in coldness, or in anger, or in fear, or in shame; for our eyes had been lifted up together before God, in the silent pleading of a mutual prayer—in the hour of a common sorrow. But with a faltering heart, and with a quivering lip, I told him that I could not be his wife: and though he looked on me long in silence, and with something of wonder, there was a hollowness in my voice, and a despairing accent in my words, that forbade him to urge me more.

But not so were we to part. Before he left me, he implored me to say what it was that so darkened my soul. But I was silent. The burning blush of shame rose to my cheek—shame, for the guilt of which I was innocent—a father's shame. But I could not speak it: I should have died in the utterance.

What his thoughts were I knew not. He

respected my silence, and ceased to entreat. But he pleaded so earnestly for one kind word to soften the harshness of my repulse; he prayed me so fervently to believe that, whatever my feelings were, his own would remain unaltered and unalterable, that for a moment I forgot all that he *was* to me, and thought only of what he had been.

I had turned away, full of the awful responsibility that lay heavy upon me—full of the deep consciousness of my own heart's weakness—drooping and silent under the knowledge of a love that I was forbidden to utter. But now, as he spoke of the sweet regard of friendship and brotherhood, I began to feel something like a hope that all was not lost to me. When he told me that, in my suffering and my tears—in the bleakness and unprotected loneliness of my orphan state, his arms would ever be open to defend, and his breast to shield me; *then*, for a moment, the mask fell from my face—and the cloud from my heart. I looked up into his eyes with a smile, as if I knew no grief. I yielded to the gentle force of those dear arms, which now for the first time sought to fold me in their fond embrace. My head sunk on his shoulder; and, amidst sobs that were as the rending

The Avowal.

away of life itself, I blessed him, and called him protector, and brother, and friend!

Fond words—but vain!

I saw him not again. His departure had been fixed for an early hour the next morning; and he went—alone, and in sorrow.

But my blessings went with him. My whole heart, my whole soul, followed his departing footsteps. I prayed in sincerity and truth that the cloud might pass away from *him*, and that he might forget me as if I had never been.

This was a bitter prayer for a loving heart. But it was the prayer of youth—and of a woman's youth. Men may be, and are, unselfish at times, and in the newness of existence, before collision with the world has worn away the impress they received from the hand of their Maker; but a woman has no self. This complete merging of its own identity in that of another, is not a part of man's nature: it belongs essentially to that of woman. It is not with him that all-pervading influence that it is with her. It is the very essence of her being: the pure, spiritual atmosphere of her life—the ether of her soul. She can no more exist without it, than we could live without the air we breathe. It is her all; her blessing, or her curse : her dower in this world, and her inheritance in that which is to come. If here it is her curse, there it would be her blessing. If it is her shame now, it will be her glory then. If on earth it is her gift to the creature, in heaven it will be her offering to her God.

CHAPTER X.

DESOLATION.

"My desolation does begin to make
A better life.
                    I hourly learn
A doctrine of obedience."
                        SHAKESPEARE.

THE snows of winter gradually melted away, and the spring returned in all its vivid and spirit-stirring beauty. But I no longer welcomed it. My mind was stricken, utterly, hopelessly, and, as it seemed, for ever. My feelings were deadened, and the love of life extinct within me. The change of the seasons; the beautiful order of nature; the succeeding of day to day; the morning's freshness, and the evening's calm—I knew them not. I floated like a corpse down the stream of time. Nothing in the present could quicken my pulse by a single throb. The past I shunned: for the memory of what had been only tortured by its contrast with what was. And as a child covers up its eyes from the object of its terror, so did I veil my mental vision from the contemplation of that most awful of all objects to the sorrowful—the life of the future. Like the dwellers of Mount Atlas, I could have cursed the sun at his rising and at his setting.

But this could not last. Such a mood of mind must end in one of two things—death, or a better spirit.

I was not to die. My destiny was not yet worked out; the aim and end of my being was not yet fulfilled. There were yet within me impulses and powers which I knew nothing of. The capacity to do and to suffer was latent within me, though buried and hidden. The ice was only on the surface; the volcano was beneath. The central fire was burning though unseen.

For some months I had been left wholly alone. Dorothea had been called to the metropolis to assist in making arrangements for the formation of some religious society. Her stay was prolonged much beyond her original intention; and now her return at all seemed doubtful.

Meanwhile the dreariness of my lot increased upon me. The silence and the solitude sank into my spirit. I had no aim, no object. Even the incitement to self-control was gone. My life was a blank.

What first aroused me from this unnatural state of torpor I cannot now remember. My first feeling was something like remorse for this utter abandonment of myself to grief. I began to look around me. I saw others equally stricken, equally borne down by suffering; some by poverty, some by the death of those they loved; and more by disease. I was surrounded by blessings the poor thirsted for, toiled for, and groaned for in vain. The being I loved was not taken from me by death; he existed in the same world, he breathed the same air as myself. I was not bowed down, body and mind, by sickness. What then was my grief? Was it past hope, past aid? I asked myself these questions again and again.

The ground was broken, but the seed was not yet sown. Had it been left for me to drop it into the soil, it never, perhaps, would have been sown. But the plants of surest growth are those whose seeds float in the air.

Every breath of the pure world without, every beam of the sun became a reproach to me. I wept over myself as over a fallen spirit, cast out because it had rebelled.

The sacrifice I had made of self to the good of another I had never for a moment repented. Happiness I had rendered up willingly, and for ever: but in the consciousness of having acted rightly—nobly—ought I not to have found peace? Alas! our lowly earth-born love — the little Isaac of our hearts—will not so be put away! No heavenly hand had interposed between me and my sacrifice. I had slain my best affections on the altar of duty. But I lingered before the shrine, awaiting vainly some sign of acceptance.

My thirst—my longing was for action. I yearned for some strong necessity to call me out of myself; some duty, some material for the capacities of my nature to work upon; something which should link me to my kind in community of feeling. It was not sympathy alone that I pined for; but for ties—strong human ties.

The impulse which was wanting was not long withheld. Better had it been so! The wing of the angelic spirit, drooping and wet with human tears, may never hope to soar through the dun and clouded atmosphere of the grosser earth. It may, indeed, struggle upward for a little space; only to be beaten back at last, trampled in the dust—broken— and torn—and soiled.

At last a letter came from Dorothea, saying that she had taken up her residence permanently in London, and wished me to join her there. She further gave me the necessary directions for the removal of the furniture, having determined on giving up the house, the lease of which would soon expire.

Had any one told me, a little time back, that the parting with any person or place could now give me pain, I should have smiled in bitter scorn—in miserable unbelief. But this was a pang I had not been prepared for. I was to part from every familiar haunt, every spot made sacred by the past. Here had I grown into stature, both of body and of mind. Here had my young thoughts been fed, and the hopes of my heart sustained. Here had I rejoiced; and oh! more than all—here had I *suffered*. On that sea had I gazed a thousand and a thousand times; and along the untracked waste of those barren sands had I explored the unexhausted regions of imagination. On this spot and on that, by the wood and by the wild, there rested memories, blest and holy as the blue sky that spread over all. The burial-ground of that village church, overhung by its solitary willow, and clouded by its yews and spreading cypresses, was the abode of my first friend—the grave of my more than mother. How often had I knelt beside that grassy sod and bowed down my head, and kissed it, and wept, as I once wept upon her loving breast! And these things were to be so no more!

And one thought, deeper than all these, came upon me in my wretchedness—*here* had I *loved!*

Had the precious wealth of my heart been poured out in the vilest abode of sin and desolation—a hovel by the wayside, or a garret in the gloomiest sink of a vice-inflated city—that spot, with all its hideous accompaniments of guilt and squalor, would have been to me the most sacred spot of all the earth; the shrine to which my soul would have turned in the weariest hour of its mortal pilgrimage. But here the beautiful was around me! Vice had never sullied the flowers beneath my feet; and peace and purity had shadowed me with their wings!

I took my way down to the sea. It was the last time that I was to look upon it. The moon was in her fullest light, and sent the reflex of her beauty in one unvarying silver line across the broad ocean mirror. Beautifully, in the language of the Basques, has her light been called "the light of the dead!"

As I looked up to those blue and cloudless skies, and across the wide waters, and heard the timed beating of their surges against the cliffs, I felt calmed and elevated. The spirit of the universe was abroad, and the petty griefs and struggles of humanity faded before it. My heart was lifted heavenward, and I vowed inwardly that henceforth I would devote it to a better service. I would crush within me every unworthy emotion. I would lay my bosom bare to the storms of life, and forgetting self, live only in my duties. The strongest passion of my soul should not henceforth divorce me from the gracious aspect of my mother earth. I had loved, and I must love still. *That* feeling could not be deadened till the breast that nourished it was cold in the grave. But it should no longer depress, but exalt me. It should henceforth be not the *shadow*, but the *light* of my soul.

Internally I prayed for help—for guidance. I felt lonely upon the earth. I could not shut my eyes to the darkness of the prospect before me. I knew that there was no kindly breast to support and encourage me in my onward path; and how, without this precious manna, was I to make my way through the wilderness? Kindness is the feeding-stream of all good; the "milk" of the parent, virtue. Were we never forcibly deprived of the fountain of her breast, our hearts would never be weaned from the nursing mother.

Still, I would not despair though alone and unaided on earth. He who, with God's help, sets himself to the noble task of modelling anew his moral and intellectual being, is at once the sculptor and the marble—the agent and object of his design: he works by the aid of the Perfect Hand till he becomes the perfect form.

As the comfortless hour of my departure drew near, these better aspirations grew somewhat faint, but were not quelled utterly. It was with a sinking heart that I wandered through the now desolate and unfurnished chambers, where every object I looked upon struck a chill through my breast, prophetic of future ills. My footsteps sounded hollow upon the bare floors; and the closing of a door for the last time, was like shutting out a familiar spirit. It seemed as if in deserting my household gods, their wrath was to follow after me through all time to come.

But there was no remedy. So I took my last look : and, hurrying away lest the strong memories within should force me back, I got into the carriage that was to bear me away, and buried my face in my hands as one who "covers up his head to die."

PART II.

CHAPTER I.

THE STRANGER.

"I am an humble suitor to your virtues :
It pleases time and fortune to lie heavy
Upon a friend of mine, who, in hot blood,
Hath stepped into the law."
SHAKESPEARE.

IT was not until some miles were placed between me and my late home that I ventured to uncover my eyes and to look around me.

The scene so familiar was no longer visible. The rocky barrier of the coast had given place to closely-cut thorn hedges ; the ocean was exchanged for a sea of waving corn-fields—those " bending pathways of the breeze ;" and as I felt myself whirled rapidly along the smooth level road, I gave one last long sigh to the past, and resigned myself to my fate.

The scenery I passed through was not without a melancholy interest. This was the same road I had traversed eight years before, when, a mere child and an orphan, I had passed from a desolate home to take my place among strangers. The year was then in its ripeness, as it was now; and everything wore as unchanged an aspect as if the time which had intervened between that day and this were no more than a dream.

How had my soul grown and expanded since then! It is not by years but by trials that our life should be measured. Years and sorrows alter us from what we were—but sorrows more than years. The wear and tear of mind and body is not to be recorded by the rising and setting of suns, but by the dawn and the decline of our passions and affections. We often live faster in some one year than in a whole lustre at another period.

The enthusiastic mind enters upon life and life's passions too soon. In cold regions the gardener shields his young plants from the warmth of the spring sun that they may be spared the cutting of the after blast. It were well if the human plant could be so shielded. Passion warms but to betray. In the garden of life, as in other gardens, it is the early snow which protects from the severity of the after frost.

I was now rapidly approaching the great

mart—the central point of civilisation—the heart of my native country—London. As I caught the first view of the Thames, my eyes suddenly moistened with that incommunicable feeling which the presence of any object connected with childhood invariably calls up.

If there is anything in existence the sight of which betrays the mind into an humbling sense of its own littleness in the scale of creation, it is that of a vast city. Its contemplation has upon the every-day journeyer of life the same effect which that of "night with all her stars" has upon the poetical thinker: it sets him at once beneath and above himself: it lowers him beneath his preconceived standard of his own individual significance; and at the same time raises him above self, and sends his mind abroad in search of wider sympathies. It has become a hackneyed idea that one is most alone in a crowd. The selfish man is so, assuredly; but not the world's citizen. *He* partakes in some measure the anxieties of the bustling concourse around him. He "reads the mind's construction in the face" of every human being he passes; and thus feels himself united in an intimate bond of sympathy with the hopes or sorrows of his kind.

I had now reached the suburbs. The bridge which spans the mighty river had been passed: lights, rendered star-like by the presence of a thick autumnal haze, began to glimmer fitfully before my eyes; and, presently, the whole artillery of wheels rumbling over the stone pavement and passing and repassing in constant succession, and with apparently causeless haste and clamour, announced that my journey was drawing towards its close. Piccadilly, that great leading canal, with all its freight of wealth, appeared and vanished like a dream; and now I felt, indeed, whirled all at once into the central gulf of the vast living stream.

A few moments more brought me to a small street leading from one of the squares; and here, wearied and worn out, more from the pressure of thought than from bodily fatigue, I was at last safely deposited at my aunt's door.

There was a pretence of greeting me, on the part of Dorothea, at once characteristic and discouraging. A lifeless movement of the hand—a cold pressure of the lip—and the farce of a welcome was over.

Wearied as I was in heart and mind, I had now to enter into a thousand minute particulars of the home I had quitted, of the arrangements I had made, of the directions I had fulfilled; in short, I had to go through a complete rehearsal of the melancholy part I had enacted in uprooting to the last fibre every familiar growth of that beloved soil—weeds to her, but flowers to me!

When at last the hour of twelve had struck, and I began to indulge in anticipations of a release, and of rest and quiet in the sanctuary of my own room, I was dismissed with a faint "good-night," and with a distant and mysterious intimation of some important disclosure awaiting me on the morrow, which effectually banished all hope of closing my eyes for some hours to come.

It was not until quite worn out with vague conjectures and more vague fears, that, yielding to bodily weariness, I fell asleep. But sleep is not always rest; and the dreams that haunted me were even more harassing than my waking thoughts. A constant succession of undefined images, accompanied by sounds like the rumbling of wheels—confused reminiscences of my late journey—mixed up with those torturing phantasms of awe and dread which every one has experienced in the hour of fever, but which none can describe, pursued me through the night.

The next morning I descended to the breakfast-room, jaded and spiritless; and, after a cheerless meal, awaited in silence the promised revelation.

From what I could learn, it appeared that I had been inquired for by a person of somewhat equivocal appearance. She had called at the house some days back, and requested to see me on private and urgent business. Upon hearing that I had not yet arrived, and being asked to leave any message she might have for me, she refused doing so, but said she would call again the day after that of my expected arrival. My aunt described her as a person of disreputable appearance; abrupt in her manner, shabbily and tawdrily dressed, and with traces of rouge upon her face.

While I was conjecturing the probable cause of her seeking me, and while Dorothea was debating whether it was proper that I should see her, a loud knock was heard at the door, and, on its being opened, my name was pronounced in a voice at once so commanding and so singular in its tone, that we both rightly concluded it to be that of the stranger.

The servant announced her as the person

who had called before, but without giving any name, and said that she desired to see Miss Merrick, and that she must see her alone.

I hesitated no longer, but entered the room into which she had been shown.

At the first hasty survey I took of the figure that met my view, I saw that it was indeed by no means prepossessing. She was a woman of about forty; not exactly masculine in person, for she was of rather low stature, but one of whom you might at first sight predicate something unfeminine in mind. Her face, though faded and careworn, and sunk about the eyes, wore a marked expression of firmness and decision of character; while the eyes themselves were penetrating and rapid in their movement—perfect shooting-stars of intelligence. A want of neatness was observable in her dress; there was a loose, slatternly look about it, which, added to her other peculiarities, gave the idea of one who, hurried through the troubled tide of life, had lost the sense of those smooth conventionalisms which form the superficies of more fortunate characters, and which, like the well-washed pebbles of the beach, serve to hide the ooze and slime beneath.

Altogether, although not so unfavourably

impressed as I had been led to anticipate, I could not divest myself of a certain feeling of restraint in the presence of a person so utterly different from any with whom I had hitherto associated.

She rose at my entrance; and no sooner was the door closed, than directing towards me a searching glance, she inquired:

"Your name is Merrick?"

I answered that it was.

"Dora?"

"Yes."

She continued: "There can be no mistake here; you are an orphan?"

I dropped my eyes. The blood rushed to my face as I stammered out:

"My mother has been dead some years."

"I see I am right," she said in a somewhat softened tone; then, as if communing with herself, she added: "Yes, she must be his child; the same open forehead, the eyes, the very face of his youth."

She sighed. There was a pause of a few seconds.

She then resumed: "Miss Merrick, I may have appeared somewhat abrupt in my questions; you must pardon it. I am influenced by no idle or aimless curiosity. You tell me your mother is dead. It will give you pain, but I must speak. Tell me," and she lowered her voice, "are you acquainted with the history of your other parent?"

I trembled from head to foot; but, controlling my emotion as well as I could, I answered that I knew all; but added, "Why do you ask me these things? Before I answer you further, tell me who you are, and how you are connected with me and mine."

"You are right," she said; "I have scarcely the right to question you. My name is Brandt —Sophia Brandt. I am only distantly related to your father; a sort of cousin, I believe. As children we were playfellows, and I have never quite lost sight of him since those old days. He is the only relation I have living. One must interest one's self in somebody; and there is no lasting hold on any ties but those of blood-relationship. I am a good deal changed since our boy and girl days. He, too, is altered—miserably, miserably. And it is of this I come to speak."

"He has, then, been heard of?" I faltered. "He is—where?"

"Hush! speak lower: a word might betray him—perhaps to death. From this time his life is in your hands."

"He has then———"

"Returned."

Gracious Heaven! this was more dreadful than all. Sentenced to death, but reprieved beyond all hope, he had returned from transportation, and his life was doubly forfeited: while I—a word of mine might betray him to an ignominious death. I could not speak. I felt choked.

She saw the shock I had sustained. She drew near, and, taking my hand, did what she could to comfort me.

At length, mastering my feelings by a violent effort, I asked what I should do.

"Calm yourself, and I will tell you. He is ill, and in the utmost poverty and wretchedness. Go to him. See what can be done. The sight of his child may comfort him, if it does no more. But I expect much from your influence over him. He is at times wild and reckless. In short, he is desperate; careless of life, and indifferent to death."

She then gave me minute directions for finding him in the obscure spot where he had secreted himself under an assumed name. And after fixing her eyes upon my face for a brief interval, during which she seemed to be struggling with some undivulged feeling, she took her leave; and I found myself once more alone.

I heard the door close after her; but I moved not. I felt bewildered, and knew not how to act. Yet act in some way I must, and promptly.

Should I speak to my aunt of this? I would willingly have avoided it; but it could not be. She must know it sooner or later. I could not leave the house for any time without her knowledge; and from my silence, what might she not suppose? She might even trace me; and thus lead to the consequence most to be dreaded—the discovery of my father.

I resolved, therefore, to let her know the truth; for I did her no more than justice in believing that, on a point of strict duty, she would aid me rather than prevent my acting decidedly and at once.

I now sought her, and gave her a hurried account of what had passed. But there was one point I did not touch upon; and that was, the relationship of this woman to my father.

There was to me something sacred in an affection which seemed thus to have outlived all the other interests of life in the breast of the wrecked creature who had stood before me;

and I felt that the admission she had made of her kinship with the fallen and degraded, claimed at my hands the respect due to one who, however lowered in the social scale, was yet united to me by the bonds of a common destiny.

When I thought of my father, all the repressed affections of my nature seemed ready to expand in love to him, and my heart swelled within me. The wrong he had cast upon me was forgotten now: the chafing of other ills had worn away its stain. I retained no thought but of his suffering. Every feeling of bitterness was merged in the tender relation which was henceforth to bind us to each other.

All that day I strove to raise up my spirit the better to endure whatever of new and unknown trial might yet await me. I looked back to the hour when in my silent communings with nature, and in my interpretations of her eternal voice amid the solitary grandeur of the wide-spread waters, I had vowed myself to choose through life the better part. I recalled my aspirations *then*, when no trial was before me; and I asked myself: "How *now* shall I keep that word of promise to my heart?"

CHAPTER II.

THE MEETING.

"The city now doth like a garment wear
The beauty of the morning."
WORDSWORTH.

"But how is this?
"Father, thy glance is clouded—on thy brow
There sits no joy."
HEMANS.

THE early morning mist which had hung like a pall over every object of the vast city, magnifying the proportions of some, and mellowing the harsh outlines of others, was gradually dispersing beneath the genial glow of an autumnal sun, when, taking my way through the almost empty streets of London, I found myself in the precincts of Westminster.

I pursued my way cautiously; noting, as I went, every object that had been described to me as landmarks for the direction of my course; and nervously alive to the strangeness of my position—alone for the first time in the heart of a populous city, bewildering in its extent, and thronged with human life.

Already, early as it was, a few wretched objects were crawling through the streets, evidencing the existence of the busy community which seemed only waiting a propitious hour to swarm out of the crowded hive, to fix, each one, upon its allotted ground, and to suck forth for the day its destined portion of honey or of poison; some to carry back to their homes the hard-earned sweets of patient toil; some to drink their drop of gall, and fold their wings—and die.

I stood beneath the walls of the venerable Abbey; solemn in its grandeur; grey with years; the sacred sepulchre of the great and wise; and I felt myself what I was—an atom —a mote in the beam of the Eternal Sun, floating at the mercy of the frail breath of time, even as the scattered dust of those to whose holy earth we offer up the vain tribute of a mortal's praise.

If any one spot could imprint deeper than another into the soul the lesson of corruption— corruption unrelieved by any such recorded triumphs of mind over matter as impressed themselves upon the gazer *here*—it was that to which I was now approaching.

I had traversed several small streets, and now found myself in a narrow close, whose old, broken-down houses— since demolished to make way for a wider thoroughfare and more habitable dwellings—wore a look of wretchedness, desertion and decay, which contrasted strangely with the bright blue sky overhead. The human population were here gainers by some hours of the short-lived day which had yet scarcely begun in the better quarters of the town. Women and children were busy about the dilapidated doors; and clothes, or rather rags, were hanging out to dry upon the broken palings that inclosed what once, perhaps, was a garden; now a receptacle for refuse and offal—the discarded portion of a beggar's meal. Here and there was visible the gaunt, sallow visage, and keen eye, of some despised Jew as he stood before the door of that saddest of all objects, a pawnbroker's shop. There hung the showy gown, and the bright-buttoned waistcoat, which careful hands had often and often folded and laid by for the Sabbath-day's wear. Mingled with these, and tossed in a heap together, were faded gauzes, crumpled flowers, and scraps of tinsel, dragged possibly from the scanty wardrobe of some starving actress—some wretched minister to the amusements of the herd; frail memorials of the triumphs of fame, and the nightly applause of a penny theatre! destined last to figure on the draggled train of the May-day sweep, and to be trampled in the running drain at the drunken close of the annual jubilee.

Farther on was a butcher's stall, from which the stifling odours of putridity reeked up through the pent air; air, not enough to keep untainted the unsightly flesh that dangled from the hooks, but only serving to turn it to a deeper and more unwholesome hue, where it hung, literally withering in the breath of the morning. On the filthy step sat a girl nursing a child. It lay on her lap a lifeless clod. Its head hung down over her knee; and its little blue, skinny arm beat against the ground, as the poor thing was roughly jogged up and down by its restless nurse. I looked in the girl's face—she was an idiot. From beneath the red locks of her loose, rough hair, the rayless eye looked out, glassy and meaningless. I saw her raise her hand to one of the hooks above her head. She clawed hold of a piece of meat, and, plucking from it a loose portion that dangled from the bone, conveyed it to her mouth. I sicken even now when I think of the idiot and her meal.

Shuddering, I passed on. The street led to a retired group of buildings, apparently storehouses, of which the lower part only seemed inhabited. They stood far back from the rest, and were half surrounded by a brick wall, which had once served to inclose an inner court, or lading-place, now unused, and thickly grown with rank grass, springing up between the stones. The remains of a crane jutted out from the front of the middle building, and immediately beneath it was an open loft, the door of which swung back upon its rusted hinges.

It was here that my search was to end; and turning to a woman somewhat decenter in appearance than the squalid objects I had lately encountered, I inquired for Maurice Elliott—the feigned name under which I had understood my father was concealed.

The woman looked at me suspiciously; and after carrying her eye coolly over every part of my dress—which, though as plain as I could arrange it, was yet out of place here—she pointed to an open door belonging to one

of the range of buildings, saying carelessly—
"He's not come in yet, I'm thinking."

I thanked her, and entered the room, if room it could be called. In one corner stood a bed with tattered hangings. Besides this, the whole contents of the place were a deal table, one battered chair, the rush-bottom of which was half broken through and trailed on the ground, and an old hair trunk. The poverty-stricken look of these wretched substitutes for furniture, together with the green damp that stood on the walls like fur, and the desolated aspect of things without, seen through the broken and patched panes of an old barred window, struck into my heart with a feeling of intense commiseration for the fate of my miserable parent.

I sat down, and pondered upon what was to come. It was strange what should lead him abroad at so early an hour. The truth never struck me, that he had passed the night out, and as the woman had said, had not yet returned. But I knew that Sophia Brandt would prepare him for my coming; and the tears rose up into my eyes, as I thought how little was the pleasure he could have felt at the idea of meeting for the first time his only child, when he could thus absent himself at the very moment she was seeking him in the wretched hovel he called his home, with a heart beating with all the longings of affection; and who, instead of being folded to his breast in the consciousness of support and safety, found herself all at once alone, in the midst of squalor, vice, and profligacy — the solitary inmate of four bare walls.

As I stood, buried in thought, but watching with anxious eyes every step that approached, I heard a harsh, thick voice, calling down curses upon some object that stood in the way, and looking in the direction whence it proceeded, I saw a man reeling in a drunken state, and making his way towards the house.

Seized with a sudden sense of dread, I sprang to the door in the hope of discovering some means of securing it. But the only bolt it possessed was so rusted, that it defied every effort to shoot it into the groove.

As the steps drew nearer and nearer, and my terror increased, I made a violent effort to drag the box I had noticed towards the entrance. Hardly had I succeeded, when a rude thrust was made at the door, which was pushed forcibly open, the trunk being driven back by the violence of the blow.

The drunken figure I had seen and dreaded

a moment before, now presented itself at the opening. The man stood an instant to steady himself; shaded his eyes with his hand, the better to discern who stood within; and then, entering, reeled forward, and dropped into the chair.

"So," he said, "you're come."

Could I believe my eyes—my ears? Was this the being to whom henceforth I was to give duty and reverence? to wait upon in humbleness, and to soothe into patience? I could not take my eyes off him: it was the fascination of the serpent. I stared into his bloodshot eye, at his trembling lip, and the unstable working of the muscles of his face. The more I looked, the more was I horror-struck. His voice—the harsh grating sound of his ribald curse, still rang in my ears.

Fortunately, the disgust and horror which must have been visibly pictured in my countenance was unnoticed by him. He was too much brutalised to discern anything clearly. But, as if conscious that my eyes were fixed upon his face, he hung down his head with a dogged look, between shame and stupefaction, and seemed uneasy in my presence, and as if he wished me gone.

By a violent effort I mastered all expression

of what was passing in my mind. I spoke to him kindly. I told him by what means I had become aware of his being in England, and of the place where he had secreted himself. My mother's name rose to my lips; but I could not utter it: it would have been sacrilege.

He neither replied, nor showed any signs of hearing what I said. At length, finding that all attempts to engage his attention were thrown away, I prepared to leave him, with a promise of seeing him the next morning.

As I did so, I approached and took his hand. It trembled in mine, and for a moment I felt softened. But the truth flashed upon me: it was the *drunkard* and not the *father* that spoke in those quivering nerves!

I had brought with me for his immediate relief a small sum of money. As I now offered this, he raised his head for the first time. His eyes glistened. He stretched out his fingers, and clutched it greedily. The sight of the gold so roused him, that he spoke at last; and, as the door closed upon me, he muttered almost inaudibly: "Ay, that's right—that's right! You'll come again — you'll come again?"

How I got home I hardly know. The loathsome scenes I had again to pass through were unnoticed by me *now*. A parent's degradation had rendered them familiar. I was, as it were, inured to the lowest vice—the most abject wretchedness, by that single hour's communion with one in whom sin was as a blight on the roof-tree of my own home.

I felt staggered. I could not reconcile the aspect of things as they were, with their idea as it had previously existed in my mind. I had risen from my bed that morning hopeful and trusting; I returned to it at night an altered creature. I could not pray. My confidence was shaken; my heart was chilled; my faith was gone.

CHAPTER III.

THE LOWER DEEP.

" What do mine eyes behold?
Horror and doubt distract
Their troubled thoughts, and from the bottom stir
The Hell within them; for within them Hell
They bring, and round about them, nor from Hell
One step, no more than from themselves, can fly.

Now conscience wakes despair."

MILTON.

WITH the light of a new day, much of my late bitterness of feeling was softened down, and a new idea took entire possession of my mind.

When I dwelt calmly and dispassionately upon the state of my poor father, I could not help feeling that his present degeneracy was but a natural consequence of the life he had led; and that, although deeply culpable in the first instance, all his errors since had arisen, as those of most others arise, out of the mere force of circumstance. He was, then, more to be pitied than condemned.

But, although I felt this to be the right and just view of the case, it was not without a struggle that I subdued those feelings of abhorrence towards the vice, and disgust of the vicious, which still rankled in my breast, when I thought of that drunken scene in the Westminster close.

Having so far brought my mind to contemplate the evil as it stood, divested of all colouring of the imagination, it next struck me that with myself alone rested the power to remedy that evil, as far as might be.

At the distance we lived apart from each other, nothing could, of course, be done. It was by constant daily intercourse alone that I could hope to win my wretched parent back to purity and peace. To do this I must take my place unshrinkingly by his side, for weal or woe; I must watch over him by day, that he might see I absolved myself from no duty to him; I must sleep under the same roof at night, that he might be led to feel, by the sacredness of the trust reposed in him, the natural obligation that devolved to him as the protector of his child.

My resolution was no sooner formed than I

hastened to carry it into effect. That very day, having got in a few humble articles of furniture, and made the place as habitable as I could, and having bid adieu to Dorothea, I took up my abode in the close.

It would be impossible to recount the trials that awaited me here, or the thousand heart-sinkings that beset me in the performance of the task I had undertaken.

I soon found that I had overrated the power of good over evil. Instead of proving a blessing to the lost soul whom I had thought it my highest duty to comfort and relieve, I found my presence hateful to him. He seemed to regard me as a perpetual reproach, a living witness of his debasement.

At first, although he generally came home in the same drunken state as when I had first met him, yet he would sleep in the house. But after a time he gave way to his old habits again; and I was left to pass the night in that wretched spot, alone and unprotected.

Added to the constant dread of discovery, and the thousand other causes that harassed and perplexed me, there was a mystery in some part of my father's conduct which I could not fathom. The little money I was able to furnish for our daily wants, I soon found insufficient for the bare necessities of life. What he did with it I was at a loss to conceive. Some days he would go out, after appropriating to himself a sum which would have served for our subsistence for weeks; and, on his return, not a shilling of it was left.

On such occasions he was always more harsh in his manner, more morose, more reckless than usual. A look of settled despair would fix itself upon his features; and, if spoken to, the demon that possessed him would vent itself in the bitterest curses—the most awful imprecations.

One night, when he had thus seized upon all we possessed, and left me alone as usual, the idea occurred to me that if I could ascertain by what means he contrived to dispose of these sums, I might possibly have it in my power to put a stop to a proceeding which, whatever it might be, was evidently ruining him utterly, both body and soul.

No sooner, therefore, had he gone out than, hastily throwing on a bonnet and shawl, I opened the door softly, and prepared to follow him.

While my step was yet upon the threshold, I hesitated. A feeling of compunction, a sense of shame, stole over me. Was I acting a fair and open part? Was it right to become a spy upon the actions of one to whom, however degraded, I still owed a sacred duty? I felt the demoralising effect of such scenes in the still voice of my accusing conscience. But the impulse was too strong, and I obeyed it.

We pursued our way; he staggering on with a hurried and slouching gait, and I following after, stealthily and with a guilty silence. I neither heard nor felt the gusty wind that was beating in my face, nor the dripping rain, which now, as if suddenly loosed from the clouds by the shock of a violent peal of thunder that broke overhead, was increasing into a perfect torrent. It was only when impeded in my movements by the clinging of my wet clothes round my limbs that I was aware how thoroughly I had become drenched by the violence of the storm.

Until now I had succeeded in tracing the step of my unhappy father. We had reached a retired and dimly-lighted street, when suddenly he stopped before the door of a small tavern. He paused a moment beneath the lamp that stood immediately in front of the bar, and after throwing a hurried glance around, as if to ascertain if he was observed, made a sudden dart through the passage; when, not daring to follow, I lost sight of him.

From the position in which I stood, a few yards in the rear, I observed a narrow court leading down by one side of the tavern, and into which looked one of its windows. While I was deliberating what next to do I noticed that the window all at once became darkened, as by the passing across of some person within. It directly struck me that this shadow was caused by my father's entrance into the room.

All was quiet without, and stealing noiselessly down the court, I approached the window. It was curtained, but a narrow opening on one side allowed the eye a full view of the group within.

In the centre of the room stood a table, round which were seated several men, who, with knit brows, fixed eyes, and lips firmly compressed, seemed intent upon the movements of another, who, as leader of that anxious band, was seated at the upper end of the board.

In *his* eye alone all was calm and passionless, on *his* lip not a nerve was shaken. With a steady hand, and with a pale, moveless visage, and a look of malicious and fiend-like enjoyment of the conflicting emotions portrayed in the restrained breathing and distorted features of those around him, he dealt out to them their fate—a fate involving joy or anguish, transport or despair, life or death, which hung upon—the turn of a card.

In another part of the room sat, stood, or crouched, in various attitudes of despair, those whose turn had already come, whose chance was past. Of these, the knotted veins, dilated eyes, and ground teeth of some; the drooping lids and hanging lips of others, presented a scene which has no parallel save in the innermost and most hidden wards of some asylum for lunacy. These were the victims of despair —these were the *melancholy mad*. It needed not the straw crown upon the head to paint them as beyond the pale of the sane and happy of their kind; the tangled, matted hair of the careless, abandoned gamester, stood out from every head, distorted by the frenzied hands that had clutched and strained it from its roots in the agony of desperation.

Towards the *first* of these groups now approached my miserable parent. This was but the preparatory step which was to lead him on to the *second*.

He took his place—the seat left vacant by the last-despatched victim. He flung down his precious gold—the idol of his heart—and with elbows resting on the table, and chin supported by both hands, firmly clenched, awaited his turn in silence.

It came. The card was dealt.

Ere it was turned up, his fingers relaxed; his hands were thrown forward, in eager anticipation of the grasp that was to make his own the doubled stake for which he thirsted.

The card was reversed.

He bent forward and started slightly. His fingers returned to their former position. He shrank within himself; but there was no hesitation, no faltering of purpose.

Again his hand was thrust into the breast of his coat. Again, more gold—and more—and more, was drawn forth. Again hope, peace, safety, life itself, were staked—and lost!

Suddenly he leaped up from his seat with the fury of a demoniac. I watched him like one spell-bound. I saw his eyes, bloodshot and strained from their sockets, rolling from side to side, now down to earth, now up to heaven, as if the utter desperation within him sought in vain for some object on which to vent its fury. At length they turned, full of revengeful fire, upon the cold, moveless gaze of him who presided at that fearful board. No second glance was needed. It was the climax of his fury, and raising his clenched hands wildly above his head, he uttered an awful curse, and with one quick bound sprung towards his destroyer.

A convulsive feeling seized my throat: I could endure no more. The dread of murder lent me wings : I flew down the passage to the door of the room. One burst and it was opened, and I stood amongst them.

Had a messenger of wrath suddenly descended from heaven into the abode of perdition, the panic could not have been more complete. But I saw nothing, heard nothing, but the wretched being I came to save; I only felt that the space cleared round me as by a spell. No resistance was offered, and I rushed at once to the spot where my father stood.

I had sprung to his side, with an indistinct idea of dragging him away. But the look which now met my eye paralysed me. It was so awful, so inhuman, so unmixedly ferocious, that I involuntarily shrank back, gasping faintly, " Father, father !"

He stood up, and with one blow of his strong arm sent me reeling against the wall. Stunned and sickened with the blow, I sank on the floor as, calling down the most dreadful maledictions on my head, he burst out of the room.

Bewildered and stunned as I was, giddy, and trembling in every limb, the sense of my position overcame every other feeling, and having made my way to the door unmolested, I found myself once more in the open air.

I now breathed more freely; but I felt so shaken that I could not walk, and, crawling a few paces away from that 'dreadful den, I sank down hopelessly on the bare pavement, and groaned aloud.

CHAPTER IV.

THE PORTICO.

" Now is he false, alas !
Almighty God! of truth the sovereign,
Where is the truth of man ?   Who hath it slain ?
She that them loveth, shall them find as fast
As in a tempest is a rotten mast."
CHAUCER.

SCARCELY had I rested my failing limbs, when the sound of approaching steps filled me with new terror, and I got up and pursued my way.

But whither to go? It was with difficulty, even though inquiring my route at every step, that I could find my way home. Home! Where was my home? Could I return to brave the fury of an enraged father—of a ruined and maddened-gamester?

But where to turn? I thought of Dorothea; and, cold and narrow-minded as she was, she appeared to me an angel of light after the scene I had witnessed; and to her I resolved to go.

The rain had now ceased, and I made my way, though with some effort, in the direction of my aunt's residence.

As I approached the Haymarket, a blaze of light from the portico of the theatre fell upon my soaked and disordered dress. Conscious of the construction that might be put upon my appearance, in such a guise, alone, at so late an hour of the night in the streets of London, I avoided passing through the crowd that issued from the portal, and was about to cross to the opposite side of the road, when my eye happened to glance across the piazza.

Leaning against one of the pillars, jaded and exhausted, stood a woman, whose gaudy dress, seen from beneath a cloak which had been hastily thrown over it, showed her to be an actress. In this woman I recognised Sophia Brandt.

From her my eye instinctively turned to the person with whom she was conversing. At her side—his head drooping—his face forced into an expression of whining sycophancy—his whole aspect betraying a servility the most abject and despicable, stood—my father!

I stopped a moment to survey them. She drew a purse from her pocket, and gave it to him. Without a word of thanks, without a single look of acknowledgment, he hurried off, doubtless to seek the pandemonium he had so recently quitted. The woman remained, looking after him. An expression of bitterness, mingled with something like contempt, stole over her features. I thought, as she turned away, a sigh heaved her breast.

My eye had wandered from her for the space of a second. I looked again. A strange figure stood before her. The expression I had marked so lately had passed away. She was talking vehemently, and in a loud tone. She laughed a harsh laugh, and with a toss of the head, turned again into the theatre.

An incessant commotion was now kept up by the arrival of carriages in every direction, It was the benefit night of a favourite actress, and the theatre had been filled to the roof.

In the midst of the din and bustle of locked wheels, squabbling coachmen, and disputes for precedence, I was suddenly arrested in my endeavour to make my way through the crowd, by a sound that thrilled to the very depths of my heart.

It pierced and transfixed me like an arrow: —it was the voice of Francis!

I turned towards the point whence the sound had issued. There he stood, full in the doorway, beneath the portico of the theatre. A young companion was at his side. Both were full of mirth : the light jest, and the lighter laugh, passed in quick rebound from one to the other. From the face of his friend the joyous spirit of youth and happiness shone out : but from the face of Francis it was not so. There was a reckless abandonment in his whole air ; a wandering feverish light in his eye, which spoke plainer than words could speak, that his heart was not in that scene—in that place. I watched him when his friend turned for a moment aside. His whole aspect changed. The smile vanished from his lip. There was that startling transition from mirth to gloom—that sudden extinguishing of its lamp by the poor benighted human worm, which is only seen where the breast is ill at ease.

The carriage he had waited for drove up. He returned into the theatre.

I lingered. That night's adventures, so full of deep and changeful import to me, I was determined to await to the end.

In a short time he returned ; but not alone. A beautiful girl leant upon his arm. Her face was radiant with a proud pleasure. A crescent of pearls lay on her forehead, shamed by its whiteness. He bent down his head, and whispered in her ear. She coloured slightly, and with a gracious but somewhat stately inclination stepped lightly into the carriage.

Scarcely aware of what I did, an irresistible impulse seized me to draw nearer, so as to obtain a better view of the lovely face of which I had thus but a passing glance.

I approached close to the window, and fixed upon her face a look destined to stamp every feature indelibly upon my memory. At this instant Francis himself leaped into the carriage; and, in turning towards the open window to draw up the glass, his eye encountered mine.

The recognition was complete; for he turned pale as death. He made an effort to stop the coach which now began to move on. It was too late: his voice was drowned in the uproar.

Away it rolled. Beauty, and youth, and health; wealth, and pride of place; all things that are honoured by men, and worshipped of the world, passed away. The gorgeous dress —the jewelled coronal—the dazzling lights— the heraldic blazonries—sunk from my sight like the going out of a beacon; and I stood alone—in dust and ashes!

A feeling, as new as it was strange, took possession of my breast. I did not ask myself what it was: but it was something more bitter than I had ever yet experienced.

My purpose was changed. I retraced my steps. Why should I seek for peace? What had *I* to do with *home?* No; I would go back to my wretchedness: I would grovel with the meanest and most lost of my kind. Pollution seemed to rest wherever I turned my eyes. The one green spot in my memory was blasted.

That night a scorching fever dried up my veins. For days I lay a helpless, gasping wretch, my body bowed down by sickness, my mind wandering in delirium.

I seemed abandoned by all, when succour came to me in my loneliness.

There was a child, a girl of eight years old, who had been my comfort in that place of desolation. She was a little stray flower from the meadows far away: a creature whose life, hitherto, had been made up of field-wanderings and village pastimes;—now, all at once, transplanted into the abode of a London huxter.

She wore on her cheek a flush born of the breezy hills. Her soft hand folded round one's fingers like the shutting of a night-flower's bells. No infection caught from the loathsome sink into which she was thus early thrown, settled upon her healthful thoughts. The blue of her native heaven was mirrored in her eye, and its purity in her heart. A meek and tender, but a dim, mysterious, fairy-like expression breathed from her face; and as she bent over me in the watchful ministry which was the silent language of her gentle and loving nature, she seemed like some being of a brighter world sent down in mercy to chase away the shadows that gathered over this.

CHAPTER V.

THE PESTILENCE.

> " The homes of men
> Were now all desolate, and darkness there
> And solitude and silence took their seat
> In the deserted streets, as if the wing
> Of a destroying angel had gone by."
> PERCIVAL.

> " So fare the many; and the thoughtful few,
> Who in the anguish of their souls bewail
> This dire perverseness, cannot choose but ask,
> Shall it endure?
>   Shall that blest day arrive
> When they whose choice or lot it is to dwell
> In crowded cities, without fear shall live
> Studious of mutual benefit?"
> WORDSWORTH.

HEALTH returned not; but the fever in part passed away, and I began to look around me once more with a sane mind.

The dreariest season of the year had set in; autumn was passing into winter. A contagious disorder was beginning to show itself in the worst quarters of the town. No sooner had it

The Pestilence.

made its appearance than it advanced with rapid pace. The abodes of the idle and the uncleanly were the scenes of its first ravages; and through the dismal close where I lingered out a miserable existence, it spread with the speed of fire through a parched forest.

Day by day the pestilence increased. A constant cloud, deepening toward night into a fog, thick and stifling as an Egyptian plague, hung overhead. Silence, unbroken save by the everlasting toll of the death-bell, reigned within and without the dwellings of the dead and dying; while, amongst the survivors, the stupefaction of despair made them seem, as they walked abroad upon the earth, almost as corpse-like as the forms that rotted beneath; till the sleep of the living became more awful than the sleep of the dead.

That such scenes should have an engrossing and absorbing interest for one who was but newly, as it were, rescued from the very grasp of death, is scarcely to be wondered at. It was something better than the mere vulgar craving for horrors, for excitement, that now led me to look intently upon the life that breathed—or rather gasped, on every hand, about my path. It is probable that I might, in happier days, have shrunk from such fellowship: but my present lot had cast me, as by a fate, into the darker places of the world—among the stern and gaunt realities of life; and, emerging as I was, slowly, out of pain into a renewed existence, I paused and looked around me to see if out of that darkness light might be struck.

I was yet very feeble; weakened in body, and with scarcely the energy of mind needful for the formation of new plans or resolves for the future. My spirit for the time was broken; but still I longed for action, or rather for the capability of acting. It occurred to me that, subdued as I was, and unfit for any continued exertion of body or mind, I might still be of some use to the wretched beings I saw around me. Much as I had heard *talked* of poverty, I had never till now met it face to face; never known more of its sting than belonged to the mere absence of wealth. Here a new chapter in the history of man was opened to me, and I could not pass it by unread—dared not say to my own soul—" What is this page of humanity to thee ?"

Far from finding my advances repulsed when, on being once more able to move abroad, I sought the dwellings of those with whom I had a fellowship in suffering, my offers of personal assistance were, in most cases, gratefully accepted. I had no difficulty, therefore, in gaining access to the abodes of poverty and wretchedness by which I was encompassed, and in studying the phases of human life, as they were here presented to me, devoid of that veil with which civilisation, in the better ranks, hides man from his fellowman.

The first house I sought was that where lived the parents of the child who had so tenderly nursed me during my illness, and to whose ministry, together with the occasional aid of her mother, I owed my life, helpless and otherwise untended as I was.

They were a family of Irish Catholics, one out of many such in that poverty-stricken and over-crowded neighbourhood. Miserable, however, as they were in all things else, they were better cared for than most of the Protestant families around them in one important respect. If their bodies were starved, at least their souls were fed. They, and others of their creed, were under the constant and vigilant supervision of the most devoted priesthood the world has ever known. To these sainted Fathers, and to the self-denying Sisters of Charity, whom I continually met in my dreary rounds, was owing all the light that broke through and illumined the darkness of that miserable time.

If I pause here for a passing moment to indulge in an inadequate expression of the admiration with which the sight of their ministrations filled me even in those my unawakened days, it is but a tribute due to a sublime self-devotion, the moving soul of which I could at that time but feebly comprehend. As day by day they passed and repassed me on their errands of mercy, they seemed to me to be creatures of another sphere than mine—angelic visitants, whose serene aspect no earthly passions could disfigure, no disturbing *self* could mar. Christ's were they, not in their words only, but in their lives: Christ's own, and Christ's only.

Crowded together in a single room, of a size which those who are accustomed to the merest decencies of life would have considered too close and unwholesome for a single occupant, I found the entire family, consisting of the parents, an aged woman, the mother of the man, and their four children. One wretched bed, if bed it could be called, which was composed of a few rags huddled together on the floor, served for them all. Two of the children—one, and the fairest of whom was my poor little favourite, already mentioned as having passed her previous years away from the city, and who had been brought up by an aunt, since dead—were in the last stage of the fever. Another, and apparently the eldest, lay a corpse in the midst of them, the coffin resting upon two chairs within a few inches of the bed where the others were passing out of life. Here, by the lifeless remains of its brother, played—as only the children of the very poor do play, especially the *city* poor—with a heart and a step alike joyless and unchilded, the last and only one of the four yet untouched by disease.

Of the two already signed and sealed for death, my little woodland flower was the first to perish. I stood by her side when her tender spirit passed away. She was dreaming of the green fields she had left behind, and her prattle was of woods and flowers. Her sense was drinking in the odours from the bean-field at the end of the little garden paddock—the ripple of the brook waters trembled into her ear. Her pale hands moved to and fro;—she was weaving in thought fairy-chains of the golden kingcups.

She died. They buried her in a pit heaped up with putrefying bodies, over which a little earth was shovelled, in that noisome place—the churchyard of a city. The solitary candle that lighted her to her last-resting place, was extinguished by the noxious gases that exhaled and steamed up into the faces of the mourners as they lowered her into her grave. A few hasty words were muttered over her coffin as "dust" was given to "dust;" and she from whose clay flowers should have sprung was left to fester almost beneath the eyes of her parents, poisoning the air they breathed.

In another close room under the same roof I found a woman living the life of a solitary in the midst of this crush of existence. She was one who, herself an humble agent in the extension of the luxuries which harden and the pleasures which corrupt, stood as a type of the living sacrifice that goes on daily in the under current of that society whose vast stream carries on its upper wave the shows of pomp at the expense of her slaves. Still young, but with a bloodless cheek, the once healthful girl—the milliner's apprentice, now nearly deprived of sight from the nature of her occupation, was reduced to seek the means of subsistence yet lower, if possible, in the scale of misery; to take up her abode with the poorest of the poor, and to gain her bread by such chance and ill-paid work as fell in her way, too wasted in body and in mind to be any longer capable of undergoing the hardships to which her earliest youth had been subjected. Through years of such bodily suffering to herself as would make the life of the galleys a relief in comparison, had her hands multiplied the sources of enjoyment to others. Hour after hour, and day after day —ay, and night after night, with little time allowed for food, and less for sleep—had she bent over her work, the embroidered robe of the peeress, the delicate white fabric which arrays the bride at the altar, or the splendid habiliments, enriched with silken traceries of various device, with which wealth *half* mourns for its sons. Through the hours of those long nights—at first, and before the keen sense of deprivation was deadened and the frame worn out—what visions must have stolen over the mental eye, and haunted the fancy of the young girl, how the breast of the woman must have yearned! Mere vanity, common to all, but looked upon almost as a grace in the rich, while a crime—as it is too often its inducement— in the poor, must here alone have ministered to pain. But besides the longing of the eye, as it wandered over the gorgeous work growing beneath the hand, there were other and intenser longings—those of the *heart*. What wealth was squandered upon a single article of wear by those whose pride was fed, and whose home blessed by the wearer! What a world of love must exist, but not for her, and others like to her! All *her* gain—yet she a woman, too, capable of love, tender-hearted, duteous, with a soul of charity that shamed the slow givers of mere alms—all her gain was the hard-earned crust bought with the life-blood from those pale cheeks!

And now that the fever took hold upon her, she felt that all was over; for sickness, an evil to all, is *ruin* to the poor. She knew that the work which, upon a lingering malady seizing her, she was incapable of applying for, would be given to others; and that, if she recovered, she must starve.

This apprehension did its work. What disease failed to do, wretchedness and the world's neglect to redress, effected; and the life which the universal slayer might for a time have spared, Poverty—the Azraël of the lowly—wafted out of the reach of more pain.

Many a scene did I witness which would sicken the soul to recall. Among other sufferers, the poor idiot I had seen on my first approach to this place of desolation, more than once crossed my path. The child I had seen her nursing was no longer with her. It had probably fallen a victim to disease ; and, now, her sole occupation seemed gone. She trod those wretched streets with a listless gait and vacant eye, apparently half-starved, and miserably clothed. I more than once spoke to her ; offered her food, which she took eagerly ; and questioned her, in order to discover, if possible, whether she was in reality as utterly forlorn and lost as she appeared. But the only sign of intelligence she showed was upon my once asking her if she had a father or mother living. She turned quickly round, as if in search of some accustomed object of interest, but newly missed ; and, as her looks were directed towards the ground, I conjectured, what was no doubt the case, that she was seeking for her little charge, on whose young lips alone, it is probable, she had ever heard those sounds of love and home. But I lost sight of her from that day; for my ability to go abroad was soon at an end.

On one occasion, while returning to my own dwelling, after spending the greater portion of the day in the closest and most unwholesome of the abodes of penury and sickness, I lingered near the bridge to witness the funeral of a waterman, whose corpse his late companions were conveying to a churchyard on the banks of the river. The coffin had been deposited in an eight-oared cutter ; and now—for the boat was on its return—the seat which the deceased had been accustomed to occupy was left vacant, and the oar which he had once pulled so vigorously, timing each stroke to the rude rhythm chanted by those of his class, was, with a piece of crape attached to it, laid across the boat. A funeral of this kind on the water was new to me, and I watched the retreating boat till I could see it no longer.

On reaching home I found myself suffering under a slight relapse of fever, the consequence either of the pestilential atmosphere I had been breathing for hours, or of cold caught while lingering on my way during the damps of the closing twilight. The effect of this renewed attack of illness, though it was by no means severe, was a return of such extreme weakness as prostrated me for the time, and totally withdrew me from any active service towards the sufferers around me.

CHAPTER VI.

THE LOFT.

"——— Years, alas! to have received
  No tidings of an only child;
To have despaired and have believed,
  And be for ever more beguiled;
Sometimes with thoughts of very bliss!
I catch at them, and then I miss;
Was ever darkness like to this?"
                                        WORDSWORTH.

THINGS were in this state, when one night I sat crouching, sick and chilled, over the embers of a few stray fagots, which were all I had been able to procure in the way of firing. Living creature there was none near me, save a little orange-spotted lizard that came and fixed its bright eyes upon me through a hole in the wainscot.

As I sat pondering heavily, the door was pushed suddenly open—and Sophia Brandt stood before me.

To look upon a human face that had a show of kindness in it, was cheering. One touch of sorrow makes "the whole world kin:" as our eyes met, we understood each other at once.

Her mission now, as formerly, was one of charity. It was not in my nature to reproach her for the misery which she had unconsciously brought upon me. But she saw it. She seemed startled by the change that had taken place in my appearance since we last met.

I was about to ask her if she knew what had become of my father; for I had not seen or heard anything of him since the night I traced him to the gaming-house.

"Say nothing about him," she replied; "I know it all. This must go on no longer. I have hit upon a scheme; but am not quite sure yet how it is to be managed. But, come, you must assist me: so cheer up. Good heavens! how pale you are! See here, I have brought you some physic."

So saying she drew from beneath her cloak a small jug containing some wine.

Her rough kindness so touched me that, between weakness and emotion, I felt so unnerved it was with difficulty I could swallow a few drops of the draught she offered to my lips.

"And now," she continued, "let me tell you

what I have planned. There is now lying in the river a vessel about to sail for America. It waits but a favourable wind. What I mean to do is to employ all the persuasion in my power to induce your father to go out there."

Seeing the hopelessness expressed in my countenance, she went on :

"Do not interrupt me. You think this impossible, I see. But I do not. I know your father better. All the inducement to remain here is the power of spending his days and nights in the gambler's hell. Now, since I discovered this—which was only a night or two back, though I have suspected it long—I have taken the only effectual means of putting an end to it. In fact," she added with a smile, "I have stopped the supplies."

"If this were possible," I said ; "but——" I hesitated. A feeling of delicacy forbade me to go on. She saw this.

"I know what you would say. You have no means—no money, and nothing to make it of. Of course you have not : but I have ; so that makes all even. You know—but, by-the bye, perhaps you don't know—that I get a better salary now than I did when I first went on to the stage. I perform six nights out of every seven at the Haymarket; now as a waiting-maid, now as a duenna, sometimes even as an empress when she has not much to do. One can look the character well enough, you know, till one comes to speak. But this is somewhat foreign to the matter: only it is necessary to explain how I come by so much money. You doubtless think me about the least likely person in the world to become a miser; but you are mistaken. I have hoarded for years—for a purpose all but hopeless. Besides the savings of my nightly salary, I have some trinkets which I could never bring myself to part with; most of them gifts in old times. Altogether I have a tolerable sum at my disposal. With this I can pay your father's passage out, as well as that of another person who might accompany him; and also set him forward a little in the New World when he gets there. *You* would not go with him?"

"Yes," I answered, "there I may be of use; here I have not a single tie." My voice trembled.

"Come, come, let us hope the best, then. If you should really decide on going, nothing can be easier than to accomplish that."

She paused and remained some time silent. I could answer her no further. I felt bewildered. There was something in her manner and speech—an apparent levity, mixed up with all her kind intentions—so strange at such a time, and in such a place and scene, that it jarred upon the mind. Better experience of human nature has since taught me to judge with more tolerance than I then could, and to look upon this seeming recklessness under the pressure of strong excitement, as one of those phases of feeling which must have been experienced, at one time or other of their lives, by many another besides poor Sophia Brandt.

After regarding me intently, and perhaps divining something of what was passing in my thoughts, she proceeded :

"We are oddly thrown together here, Miss Merrick ; you, reared and fitted for the better ranks of society ; and I, born to nothing but what I am—and not much the better for the life I lead. You have a troubled lot to go through yet, I fear : my days of heart-ache are over ; Heaven be thanked for that, at least! They tried me sorely while they lasted."

She ceased, and sat looking thoughtfully at the dead ashes, for the fire was gone. At length, as if a sudden thought struck her, she raised her head quickly, and continued in a more hurried tone :

"You must not judge of me by what you

see me now. I have nothing to reproach myself with. We poor actresses—especially of the lower grade—are exposed to terrible temptations, and I fear we are judged more hardly than we deserve. It is a cruel mistake. Among my sisters in the craft, there are few—very few—we women need blush for. Then, all are wonderfully charitable. The profession itself has its nobler side, too; its devotion to art, which some of us make almost a religion. I could have done so once. But that is all over now.

"My story is soon told. I took early to the stage; soon found that I had little power to express what was in me, and failed to get on. In short, I could not earn enough to keep my poor mother, whose days were numbered. What did I do? Well, badly enough; yet I suppose I might have done worse. There was a poor scene-shifter who asked me to marry him. So I became a wife. But it turned out miserably. The man was a brute. He took my small earnings, and beat and bruised me almost out of life.

"Well, I became a mother. God knows how I loved my little one; but my sole comfort was soon lost to me—such as it was, for, owing to the ill-usage I had endured, the child was not quite right in its mind. It was taken from me in a rage one day, and sent I knew not where, though I had reason to believe it was hidden somewhere in this neighbourhood; and I have haunted the place from time to time ever since, but in vain.

"For years I have had but one object—to find this child; and have lived poorly and lodged miserably for its sake. But I could obtain no direct clue. Its father had left me long; and he alone knew what had become of it. Yet, do you know—it is foolish of me—but I somehow think I shall find it yet. There was a birthmark upon its throat—two or three blue spots, like a link of glass beads; its hair, as a child, was inclined to be red. Besides this, although it must now be sixteen—seventeen—eighteen—no, seventeen years old, I am sure I should know it at once for my own. My poor little Sue!"

She stopped. A melancholy quiet seemed to pervade the room, as we now and then interchanged a few syllables, and again relapsed into silence.

At last she got up to leave me. She was on the point of giving me, before she went, some directions how to proceed, in order to obtain my father's consent to leave England, when a sound overhead, as strange as it was unaccountable, made us both start, and put a stop to what she was saying.

We listened: all was still again. The noise had evidently proceeded from the loft above. It was a sudden crash, followed after an interval by a shuffling, scraping sound, like the dragging of some weight across the floor.

We remained standing in the same position, silent, doubtful, and awaiting in some trepidation the recurrence of a sound so mysterious at such a time and in such a place; but nothing stirred.

Hardly, however, had we dismissed the subject from our thoughts, when we heard it a second time. Drag—drag, it went across the ceiling: and this time the shuffling was accompanied by a noise of another description; something between a yell and a moan—an indistinct, maniacal sound—a low guttural intonation, like the babble of idiotcy.

There could no longer remain a doubt that some one had made their way into the loft; but for what purpose it was impossible to conceive.

What was to be done? We looked at each other, but neither had power to speak. It was at this moment that the cry we had heard was renewed, but in a tone somewhat different; and for a moment I fancied I was familiar with the sound. It continued at intervals; and the more frequently it was repeated, the more convinced I felt that I had heard it before. All at once it occurred to me—surely it was the voice of the idiot girl!

No sooner had the conviction seized me, than I was on the point of communicating it to Sophia Brandt; but as I looked up into her face, in the act to do so, the expression I saw there restrained me. Her head was turned in the direction of the sound, to which she listened breathlessly. For a moment, while I still contemplated her, the shadow of some deep inward thought seemed to pass over her face. It was as if the cloud of a coming woe were brooding above her. She seemed unconscious of it, and it passed as it came. But not so its effects upon myself; a rush of strange thoughts, a crowd of terrible images, broke in upon my mind.

A singular coincidence was suggested between the tale she had just related to me, and the existence of this idiot girl, and her apparently desolate, unfriended condition; here, in the very neighbourhood which the child-seeking mother had haunted for years, with the vague yearning of a hope which was but a better name for despair. Could it be? Was the mystery to close here, at once and for ever?— The issue was nearer than I dreamed.

CHAPTER VII.

THE LOST FOUND.

> "On that woeful day
> A pang of pitiless dismay
> Into her soul was sent;
> A fire was kindled in her breast
> Which might not burn itself to rest."
> WORDSWORTH.

AS soon as I had recovered some degree of self-possession, my first impulse was to solve this mystery, alone, if possible. But how to prevail on Sophia Brandt to leave me, I knew not. I feared to urge this, lest, in so doing, I should betray what was passing in my mind. There was clearly nothing to be done but to let things take their course, and to trust that the idea which had so suddenly possessed me, was but a wild freak of the fancy to which the tale I had just heard, together with the alarm and its consequent excitement, had given birth.

Although the sounds had gradually lessened, they had not ceased; and, as we could neither of us rest under the uncertainty as to their cause, we at once agreed that the place must be searched.

It occurred to me that, at the back of the building, there was another room, adjoining the one which I had converted into a sleeping chamber for myself, over which the same loft extended. From this, the ceiling being in many places entirely broken away, we could, with the assistance of a table and chair, climb sufficiently high to see, or at least to hear, what was going on above.

We now, therefore, stole noiselessly out of the room we were in, and bearing a table and chair between us, proceeded to the one in question.

As we looked upwards through the broken rafters we could feel the cold night air rushing through the opening, and it then first struck me that the loft door must be open. I remembered, also, to have seen a workman's ladder resting against the adjoining building; and this, it appeared plain, had afforded the means of ingress.

I trembled so violently, and my head swam to such a degree, that I found it impossible to stand on the chair without being in danger of falling; and Sophia Brandt, seeing the state I was in, herself mounted to the opening.

I asked, in a whisper, what she saw.

"I don't know," she replied in the same tone: "but don't alarm yourself. There is something moving at the farther end; but there is such a fog I can't make out what it is. Hush! Listen! It moves again; I see it plainer now. It is coming this way."

The thing was silent, but the dragging motion continued. I heard something drop, and looking up, saw a long, lean, emaciated arm protruding through the rafters.

Sophia Brandt, who had continued to watch the creature, whatever it was, now leaped down from the chair with a sudden exclamation.

"Get a light," she cried; "it is some wretched thing. My blood curdled as I looked at it. Are you afraid? We'll go together."

We went back together to the room we had left, and returned with a candle.

I then held the chair and lighted her, while she climbed into the loft. She approached the object of her search, and stood over it for a moment. She then knelt, and bending down her ear, seemed to be listening. She appeared satisfied; and now, placing her hands beneath it, she proceeded to lift it up and carry it towards the opening, through which she crept, still bearing it in her arms.

A moment more and she had descended. She laid down her burden. The form was a woman's, and, although young, wearing a look of age and decrepitude that did not belong to its years. As I bent over it with the light I at once recognised the face. The features were distorted by pain and suffering. One of the legs was broken, and wrenched out of its position. The tangled red hair streamed back from the forehead. It was the idiot girl.

A pang shot through my heart as I thought that this forlorn creature had probably watched me in some of my recent wanderings, and, tracing me home, had sought, with little better than brute instinct, for the hand that had fed her. From her broken limb it would appear that having, by means of the neglected ladder, climbed up to the door of the loft, she must have fallen from its ledge on to the floor beneath, thereby occasioning the sound which had first alarmed us.

The poor thing remained perfectly quiet where we had laid her down. She was evidently dying, partly from want and partly from the injuries she had received while thus in search of food and shelter. The only signs of life remaining were a convulsive twitching of the muscles and now and then a faint wail.

From the piteous object before me, my attention was recalled to Sophia Brandt. From the moment when she had deposited her burthen at my feet she had uttered not a word. She continued bending over the girl, her eyes fixed upon her face, perfectly moveless.

All at once, as if confirmed in some vague idea that had taken possession of her mind, she again knelt down by the dying idiot, and with a quick motion, putting back the hair from her forehead with both hands, bent her eyes upon its face more fixedly than before. She next hurriedly removed the covering from its throat, and in doing so exposed to view a livid stain beneath the right ear—four small blue dots; the very marks she had described to me but an hour before!

No sooner had she discovered these, than a slight gasping sob burst from her lips; and, pressing her hand upon her forehead, as if to still the pulses that were throbbing there, she stared vacantly round the room.

At last, as if for the first time conscious of my presence, she raised her eyes to my face with an expression perfectly startling in its wrung look of anguish, and waving her arm in the direction of the room we had left, gasped out, "The wine—wine!"

I ran back in search of it, and returned with the jug. With a shaking hand she attempted to pour some of the wine down the poor creature's throat. But it was of no use; the life of the idiot was almost gone. A few seconds more, and without a sigh, without a look of recognition, the features settled into the quiet of death. An expression of child-like meaning stole over the face; the blank look of idiotcy had vanished. The soul that had been forcibly wrested from the poor human clay by unkindness and neglect, returned for an instant to its mortal habitation, again to abandon it at once and for ever.

The wretched mother watched the feeble life go out. She had folded her arms round her lost child, and supported its head upon her breast. But when she saw the eye grow glassy, and the jaw drop, as the last spark of life became extinct, she suddenly put it from her. And now the passion of her strong nature was indeed awful.

She bit her lip till the blood sprang. She beat her breast, and screamed in one violent and continued paroxysm. She tore her hair; she raved till the empty desolate building rang with her dreadful agony. I attempted to hold her, but she darted from me and flew about the room like one possessed.

After a time the strength of her passion completely wore itself out, and she sank down on the floor, helpless as a child. Then, for the first time, tears came to her relief; but *such* tears! they were awful to witness—sudden, gushing, overwhelming.

I let the storm take its course, but when it had somewhat subsided I tried to lead her away. She was quite passive, and supporting her to my own sleeping-room, I drew her gently towards the bed, and she lay down.

She never spoke the whole of that night. I watched by her side, but her face was turned towards the wall. A few broken sobs alone betrayed the anguish within, and when these ceased I was uncertain whether or not she slept, she lay so still. But I think she could not have closed her eyes; for once, when the first dawn of the morning shone through the broken panes at the foot of the bed, she looked suddenly round at me with a face so haggard and so wild that I began to fear the agony she had endured had disordered her mind.

She turned away again, and I continued to watch her as before. I thought over all the horrors of the scene that had just passed under my eyes. This was the third meeting of parent and child to which I had been a startled witness—twice as a looker-on, and once in bitter participation. First, that of Francis and his mother, where joy had usurped the offices of grief; next that of my father and myself, in drunken debasement on the one hand, and in bewildered horror on the other. But perhaps the most awful and thrilling of all was that of the actress-mother and her idiot child.

CHAPTER VIII.

THE "GOING OUT OF EGYPT."

> " Ye powers
> Of soul and sense—mysteriously allied,
> Oh, never let the wretched, if a choice
> Be left him, trust the freight of his distress
> To a long voyage on the silent deep ;
> For, like a plague, will Memory break out ;
> And in the blank and solitude of things,
> Upon his spirit with a fever's strength
> Will Conscience prey."
>
> WORDSWORTH.

THE morning was far advanced when Sophia Brandt rose from the bed, and without turning to where I sat leaning against the wall, wearied out with my night's watch, with an unsteady step moved towards the door.

I got up, and laying my hand on the latch, and placing myself so as to intercept her, asked whither she was going.

In a voice so changed and so hollow that I scarcely knew it again, she answered, "To bury my dead."

I begged her to wait a little while, and we would go together. She made no resistance; but, as if sickening at the thought of the task that awaited her, returned again into the room.

I now laid before her some bread and a little milk. These she ate, and seeing me busied in making up the fire, lent her assistance mechanically.

This I encouraged, and continued to employ her in various little offices; thus using every means in my power to detain her as long as possible, that her mind might recover itself in some degree before she again encountered the sight of the corpse.

When at last, in spite of my efforts to divert her mind from the one engrossing thought, I saw that she was still painfully brooding upon it, I ventured to allude to the subject, and to suggest some measure in reference to the interment; but, to my surprise, I found that the poor mother had already arranged everything relative to the funeral, even to the most minute point. Through those hours of the long night, during which she had lain so quiet, it would seem that her mind had been busily occupied in settling the exact manner in which her lost child was to be buried from her sight. As she now began to talk freely upon the subject, it appeared that her great object was to have the remains deposited in some spot remote from the city. Notwithstanding the shock she must have received at the sight of the wasted and distorted form as she found it first, after so many years of separation, she still thought of it only as it had lain upon her bosom of old; and wrecked as it was, a clod which the soul had scarcely animated in life, and which lay now a crushed and sightless thing on the lap of its native earth, she could not endure the thought of its being lowered down among the crowded graves in the heart of a great city.

Many years back, in consequence of the rapidly increasing population of these "cities of the silent," burial-grounds had been established at a short distance from the bounds of the metropolis; and although, from the rapid growth of the suburbs, the distinctive character, the solitude, of these places of sepulture was already nearly lost, and the burial-grounds themselves fast becoming a portion of the city, there remained spots where yet lingered something of the original greenness of these once lonely retreats of the dead. Here it was that Sophia Brandt had determined to deposit the corpse.

Her preparations were soon made. Her first act was to seek out some of her old associates, and to consign to them such of the necessary arrangements as she had not herself courage to undertake; and few, perhaps, of those whose position in the world was far above her own, and who would have looked down upon the poor actress, could have found more of real sympathy at such a time, or more of prompt and kindly aid than was now cordially offered, and accepted with a thankful heart.

All was soon arranged, and it now only remained to take a last look at the poor clay, and to lay it down with the worm. Before it was finally hidden from her sight, the mother cut off a ragged lock of hair, and hid it in her breast. Dust was gathered to dust, and when all was over and the earth lay smooth again and there was no more to be done, we stood a moment and looked in each other's faces.

The same thought was present to both, and dropping on our knees—she at the head and I at the foot—we bowed our heads over the grave and prayed long and silently by the dead.

As if to complete the work of burial, a bell from the near church began to toll heavily. It was sounding for another, perhaps for many more; but it served for the idiot's funeral peal as well.

How different, though but a little space apart, was this burial from the last!

My little favourite—my gentle woodland girl—had been rudely thrust down amidst the corruptible and corrupting; but the poor deformed creature who had existed in the heart of such things all her crushed life, and who knew not what the breath of a flower meant, nor its name, was buried beneath pure mould, where the long grass might spring up and wave freely in the wind, and the swallow make its nest in the eaves of the little chapel above her, and skim cheerily over the surface of the rain-pools that would collect about her sod when the summer came again.

The prayer of a mother's lip—though that lip was little used to prayer—broken and formless, and audible only at intervals when the gasping sob was hushed, stole over the poor child's rest and sanctified the spot.

We rose and went our way—I to the place I called my home; but the stricken mother turned away her altered face, and, with a backward motion of the hand, took mine and clasped it strongly, and so left me.

We met soon again; but of the past neither spoke. Our talk was now only of the future.

My father came in with her one day, and I was spared all further pain on the subject, for it was settled. We were to sail for America with the first fair wind; and Sophia Brandt was to accompany us.

A few days served to complete the whole of our preparations. I took my leave of Dorothea, and we soon found ourselves on board. It all seemed like a busy dream—the vessel lying in the harbour, and we upon her deck, three homeless, houseless creatures, gazing half-bewildered upon the scene before us.

The wind that was to waft us over the broad Atlantic swelled our sails at last. Once fairly out at sea, I breathed more freely. The haunting dread which had possessed me for months was no longer present. The fresh breeze invigorated my wasted frame, and instilled new life into my spirit. My father, perhaps influenced by the presence of Sophia Brandt, or feeling at last that I had made some sacrifice for his sake, now for the first time assumed an air of something like kindness. On the whole, the change from my late condition was a great and blessed relief.

But there were long days and nights yet to be passed in the solitude of the wide waters; and thought would be busy. The peace of mind I rejoiced in was, after all, only comparative; no real blessing was added to my lot; and after a time the old wounds began to rankle afresh.

Then rose up, startling in their vivid reality, the forms and the faces, the very looks and voices, of those I had left behind. Francis— my own Francis once, but now another's— stood before me as he had stood on that fearful night, beneath the portico of the theatre. The same reckless expression passed over his face. Beside him, leaning on his arm, and almost breathing upon his breast, was that graceful girl, with her look of haughty and high-born beauty. Was she his bride—his wife?

Another thought, equally bitter, had troubled me ever since that hour. *He* had seen me, then and there; seen me an outcast in London streets, at midnight. What was I now in his thoughts? Was my place kept sacred there? or was my memory defiled to him for ever?

These thoughts harassed me not only through the day, the night became filled with them. Dreams, which were mournful realities, and to which were added other more indistinct shadows of pain and sorrow, pursued me upon the great deep. But my dreams were of *them ;*—still, always of *those two*. Scenes of strife, sometimes even of bloodshed, were mingled up with them in strange confusion. At times, I thought I was wandering about a dismantled palace, and up and down cold stone steps, and through a series of chambers one within another, till I lost my way: then I found myself all at once in a rich saloon : then it changed to a church : and, last, to an open tomb ; and within it lay a form arrayed in white, and garlanded with flowers ;—and the face was *her* face ;—and against the tomb lay the white marble slab that was to close over youth and beauty ; and it was spotted with blood-drops ; and blood, streaming about in broken channels, formed the marble's veins. Then I thought Francis came, and bent over it—looked in—and laughed.

Whenever I awoke from visions like these, and they were frequent, one question always presented itself to me :—had I done well? Had I done wisely, kindly? The world would say I had acted prudently in striving to crush within the breast of Francis the love he bore me : but had I not crushed his happiness with it ? How should I answer it to my conscience through years to come, if evil should ensue? I felt bewildered, and utterly at a loss to disentangle the mingled web of right and wrong. I seemed to have been playing at cross-purposes all my life long. I had striven after great sacrifices; and in every case the result had defeated my blind will. What if Francis, persuaded of my coldness, or believing me unworthy, should heedlessly throw away his happiness in an ill-assorted marriage? What if dislike and distrust, and heart-burnings, and ill-dissembled hate, or guilt, shame, remorse, and lasting wretchedness, should arise out of all my fancied good resolves? Such things had been, and might be again.

Often, stifled with the weight of agonising thoughts, I would ascend to the deck, and sit there for hours. As I watched the rise and swell of the waters, the heaving motion of the vessel seemed to rock me into a kind of calm. All vague and visionary fancies, affection's harmless superstitions, would there crowd in upon my mind. The solitary sea-bird that poised itself for a moment between me and the blue sky, and then alighted on the mast, was greeted as the spirit of some being I had loved and lost; and not a breeze that rose or fell moaning along the sea, but visited me like the sigh of some lone heart, withered and blasted like my own.

But I was not a solitary instance of the peculiar effect sometimes produced upon the mind by a long sea voyage. There was one into whose spirit the stillness of the unbroken waste of waters sunk with a more subduing power—a more fatal influence; and that one was poor Sophia Brandt.

We had not been many weeks at sea when a marked change came over her. Her brilliant eye, which through her greatest suffering had worn a wild and restless light, all at once was quenched. She became silent and gloomy. None knew what was troubling the springs of her life; for she communicated with none, not even with myself. Whatever it was that so wrestled with her, there was no effort, not a single struggle to overcome it: she sank at once.

One night she had taken her place, as usual, by the capstan—her favourite post. Her hands were clasped rigidly together, resting on her knees; and her dull leaden eye set fixedly upon a particular plank of the deck. It was the vacant melancholy stare of a wrecked mind; for there was nothing to attract it to that spot; nothing but the blank board.

Where were her thoughts wandering? To her wasted youth—her blighted hopes? To her early playmate; he who was with her here—whom she was here to save? To her brutal husband, and the home of misery to which he bore her? To the first feeble cry of her child; and its last miserable wail as it was torn from her with curses? To the blaze of a theatre and its applauding crowds; the nauseous, fulsome flattery—the disgusting adulation of the vice-worn and corrupt? To the midnight brawl—the coarse tavern wit—and the nightly scenes of the gamester's loss, ruin, and self-slaughter? To the Westminster close—the stifling pestilence—the death-scene beneath the loft—and the idiot's grave?

The apparently dulled sense was busy with all these, and more than these. The bosom of the wife was throbbing for revenge; the heart of the mother was bleeding for repose. The first was left to other hands: the last she found.

The steersman had turned his head aside. The last loiterer on deck had strolled towards the forecastle. She rose up slowly; looked around her like one dreaming; raised her arms above her head and—sprang!

There was a quick gruff call of "Overboard!"

and a rush to the steerage. Boats were lowered, and lights thrown out. But the waves, broken by the momentary plunge, had closed over the suicide. There was nothing — not a mark —not a trace—not a ripple on the deep; nothing but the smooth, glassy wake of the parting keel!

CHAPTER IX.

A NIGHT AT SEA.

"Lo! they come,
The loathsome waters in their rage.
Vainly we look up to the lowring skies;
They meet the seas,
And shut out God from our beseeching eyes.

"Hark! hark! Already we can hear the voice
Of growing ocean's gloomy swell;
The winds, too, plume their piercing wings!
The clouds have nearly filled their springs."
　　　　　　　　BYRON.

THE ship went on her course. The same sullen midnight wave that had closed over the living, glanced and sparkled cheerily above the dead, as it reflected the tints of the clear blue morning heaven. So vivid and dazzling were the slant rays of the newly-risen sun on all around, that the eye instinctively turned for relief to the opposite horizon, where a slight hazy belt bounded the gazer's view. A Sabbath calm seemed to rest on the sea and on the sky. Not a billow rocked the noble ship; she rested almost immovably on the ocean, breasting the waters like some huge sea-bird. Her sails hung droopingly on the yards, with scarce a breeze to stir them. Nothing spoke of life through all that wide Atlantic world, save that now and then a solitary porpoise would leap suddenly up out of the deep, falling back again with a splash, distinctly heard amid the silence that reigned around.

But lovely as was the scene, brilliant, and almost oppressive from its dead calm, it was a loveliness not destined to last.

In a few hours clouds began slowly to collect; until the sun, at first partially veiled, became wholly hidden. The wind grew fresher, and the ocean less clear. Birds, one after another, were seen traversing the air overhead, uttering shrill cries, and hastening to leeward, as if from some region of storms. These gradually increased in numbers: where before there appeared one solitary voyager, they now came in pairs. Others followed; until the sky became mottled with their outspread wings. For awhile they would wheel, eddying, round; and then again sweep off to the windward, with cries still more piercing and clamorous.

As night drew on, all on board became sensible of sudden heavings of the vessel, as she rose and sunk at the mercy of the now increasing swell. These signs of a storm still distant, were accompanied by low, fitful, shivering gusts, the creaking of cordage, and the flapping of sails against the yards ; all giving warning of the approach of a tempest about to visit us in its utmost rigour.

The gale rapidly increased. It had been gradually growing in strength ; and now came deepening on—sweeping, piping, whistling, and rushing with the speed and force of a perfect whirlwind.

At last the hurricane burst upon us in all its fury. Before the order to "reef topsails" could be obeyed, the topsails themselves were torn to shreds ; till, beneath the flapping and lashing of the unconfined sail, the mast bent like a reed.

By this time the alarm was given ; and most of the passengers left the cabin, and crowded on deck. Some even refused to return below, although repeatedly urged to do so.

This was no time for much ceremony ; yet the captain, in the midst of his arduous charge, descended to the cabin, where I still remained, well knowing that I should only be in the way on deck, and took me aside.

"Miss Elliot," said he, addressing me by my assumed name, and in his rough sea-phrase, "you are the only craft here one can deal with reasonably : try what you can do to get those squalling women below-decks. If they won't go by fair means they must by foul—tell 'em so." And he hurried off, leaving me to execute as I best could the difficult task he had imposed.

By explaining to the poor scared creatures that unless they obeyed at once, force would be used to compel them to go below, I at last succeeded ; but the scene that ensued—the eternal questions, the sighing and groans, the exclamations of fear and wonder, that assailed me from all quarters, was less bearable than the tempest that raged overhead. I would have given worlds to escape from it by taking my place amidst the utmost fury of the hurricane ; but feeling that I might be of use where I was in keeping the rest below, I made no attempt to stir.

For three days and three nights there was no abatement of the storm. Anxious looks began to be exchanged even amongst the hardy crew; and although not a word had yet escaped denoting danger, there was an appearance of thoughtfulness and reserve on the part of the captain, in which I at once saw ground for serious alarm.

At length the fatal truth could no longer be concealed. The ship was driven far out of her course; her rudder beaten off; and she had become perfectly unmanageable.

She was now almost laid on her beam-ends; and it became necessary to cut away the masts, which were immediately launched overboard. The ship then righted of herself; but the straining of her timbers by the blast had caused her to spring a leak, and all hands were ordered to the pumps. My father was called upon to assist, in turn with the rest, at this laborious work, while I still remained below with the rest of the passengers.

It would be impossible to depict the dismay, deepening into absolute despair, which seized upon those miserable souls. Most of them had left behind safe but humble homes for the chances of a sea voyage, and the uncertain prospects of the wide prairie and the untrodden forest of the New World. Some had left parents, some children, some brothers and sisters, in the land they had quitted, who were to rejoin them in the Far West when the woods should be cleared, and the hut be raised, and the waste bloom around them. Many a lip had dwelt fondly upon the meeting to come, as each separate little household group had gathered round the fire on the eve of departure. Flower seeds had been collected from the oft-tended garden-beds, and some few familiar articles of furniture had been carried away from the frequented chambers, to give to the new home a look of the old. Anticipation had been busy with the time when the farm should grow beneath industrious hands, and the flocks increase, and the pastures widen, and the board be spread, and the blazing pine-log heaped. The hope that pictured these things had been as vivid and intense as was now the despair.

All that remained to be done was to take to the boats. This was a frail chance; for although the wind had lulled, a heavy sea was still rolling; and it seemed almost impossible for a boat to put off without being instantly swamped.

But there was nothing else for it. The longboat was first lowered; and such provisions as were necessary having been hastily stowed into it, there was an eager and sudden rush to the ship's side, and in a moment the boat was filled.

So quickly had this been effected, that it seemed the work of magic. But the strong instinct of self-preservation, added to the intense fear which seized upon the unfortunate passengers, only served to hasten their fate.

One after another they crowded into the devoted barque. Amongst them, heedless that there was one on board whose safety he was bound to insure even before his own, was my wretched, lost father!

The weight suddenly pressing upon the boat, brought her to the water's edge. An attempt was made to push off; but a giant wave came foaming along. They strained at the oars with the strength of desperation; but already the boat was water-logged; and the long undulating swell of the rapidly advancing billow rolled nearer and more near. As it rose over their bows, there was one long, agonised, heart-rending shriek, and a passionate raising of despairing hands to heaven. Then followed a roaring, rushing sound of the falling wave, as it plunged over and dispersed; and a dashing upward of the feathery spray as the surf curled and spread itself over the spot —but the boat was gone!

It all passed in an instant. But, fatal as had proved this first attempt, another and another boat was quickly manned with the remainder of the ship's crew.

Besides myself, the captain was the last who prepared to leave the wreck. He was about to follow, when he espied me for the first time. Seizing me with a kindly force, he bore me to the ship's side—but the boats, one and all, had pulled off!

He called to them. They heard him. Still they strained every nerve at the oars. A show of resistance was made by a few, and an effort to steer the boat back in the direction of the hulk. But the deed of mercy was over-ruled. Both the boats—as surely doomed as that which had gone down before our eyes—were rapidly making head; and we were left to await death alone, in the sinking and abandoned hulk.

Never shall I forget the captain's look when first he fully understood that the crew had wilfully abandoned him to his fate. He was a rude, rough man, but not an unfeeling one. He had commanded these very men in many a voyage, in fair weather and in foul, in storm and in calm; they had eaten of his bread, and drunk of his cup, and he had trusted them as his own children: and now, in his utmost need, they forsook him. This was bitterer than many deaths; and the strong man sunk down upon the deserted wreck, and cried like a child!

His grief soon subsided, and gave place to anger; and he cursed them bitterly. He looked up, and seeing me at his side—"And you, too!" he exclaimed. " Poor girl—poor girl! What can I do to save you?"

"Nothing," I replied; "we must await the end."

"Well said," cried he; "we'll stay by her to the last."

But seeing some loose spars lying near, he changed his purpose, and, springing up, set vigorously to work to construct a raft. The wind was lessening, and the fury of the waves beginning to subside; so that a hope yet remained of keeping afloat for a few hours longer.

While he was thus employed, I remained looking on in silence. Until now I had borne up with a strange and almost unnatural self-possession. In the rage of the hurricane—the swell of the waters—the storm and the darkness—there was something so sublime, that nothing like a dread of death had possessed me for one moment. But now, when the seas grew calmer and the wind was stilled, and I was about to trust myself to the waves upon a few frail planks lashed rudely together, the voice of nature would be heard, and a shudder thrilled through my frame.

But it was no time for the indulgence of useless fear: and soon a new source of hope and of ultimate safety presented itself.

In the midst of his labours the captain stood up for a moment, and while casting his eyes round in search of more spars, some object in the distance arrested his attention. No sooner was he assured that his suspicions were correct, than laying his hand on my arm, he pointed towards the east, crying: "A sail! a sail!"

And a sail it was, though a distant one; and evidently bearing towards us.

The hulk had now sunk to the water's edge; and the raft being completed, we placed ourselves upon it and allowed it to float off, just as, with a sudden downward rush, the wreck disappeared, ingulfed in the waters.

Many a wave washed over our frail ark; but it bore up bravely. We had hoisted a little flag of distress, and as if in answer to our summons, the stately vessel drew nearer and nearer, till at last, as it espied us and hove-to, the feeling of sudden rescue from the grave was stronger by far than the previous despair. The grateful sense of safety stole over us both; and, for me, my eyes filled with a welcome gush of tears, which had long been strangers to them.

Nothing would induce my rough but generous companion to stir from his place until I was slowly and carefully raised to the ship's deck.

"There!" he cried, "take that girl first; she's worth a whole ship's crew—(d—n them!) She stood it manfully—manfully!"

Once on board the gallant *Etna*—which proved to be an English frigate, bearing an admiral's flag—I seemed in some danger of being killed with kindness. The "poor young lady" was to be tended and waited on by all hands. It was in vain I persisted that I stood in no need of assistance; the whole ship's company — captain, officers, crew, and all, seemed contending for the right of ministering to my wants. They seemed to regard me as some poor bird that had flown into their bosom for safety and protection from the storm that had weighed down its wings; and safety and protection I found indeed, given aboundingly, and in the spirit of the gentle and the just.

CHAPTER X.

HOMEWARD BOUND.

"Out of these blacke waves let us sail,
O wind, O wind!"
CHAUCER.

"And must we be divided? Must we part?—
Ay, hand from hand, my love, and heart from heart."
SHAKSPEARE.

WHEN it became known that on that fatal night my father had been taken from me, the tenderness with which I had at first been treated was redoubled. But were I to say that his loss weighed painfully upon my mind, should I be believed? It was not in the nature of things that it could be so. Beyond a solemn sense of the sudden and awful manner of his death, and the questionable spirit in which he had met it, my only feeling was one of unmixed relief. I had, it is true, wept much and bitterly at first; but my tears were not so much offerings to his memory as mournful oblations upon the altar of my own heart's wasted and despised affections. I grieved, not because my love had gone down with him into the deep, but rather because he had repulsed and forbidden it to expand into that full flower which even the bitter waters of death would have nourished like dew.

But he was gone. Tears availed nothing now; and I had again to bear my part in life alone, for good or for evil.

My present position was a somewhat strange one; and, under other circumstances, there would have been a charm in its very singularity. I seemed to exist in an era long gone by. The true spirit of chivalry; the pure, fervent admiration of the womanly character, bordering upon devotion, which cast a glory over the early ages, still glowed in the heart of England's navy. To the graceful, knightly air of mingled tenderness and veneration, was here added the beautiful and touching simplicity of character so essentially belonging to the British sailor.

We were fast approaching the shores of England; and as the white cliffs gradually developed themselves in the distance, thoughts of home were busy at the hearts of the homeward bound. Nearer and nearer drew our noble bark towards its destined haven.

At last, with a joyful shout the land was hailed. Amidst a scene of so much heartfelt enjoyment, it was not without emotion that I bade farewell to my late generous protectors; and as one by one they departed from my sight, I stood upon my native shore, alone— and wept.

I immediately prepared to take my way towards the metropolis, to the only home I knew—that of my aunt Dorothea. My journey thither, unrelieved by any event worthy of notice, I pass over in silence, and hasten to describe the scene which awaited me on my arrival.

On my entrance into London, I found the attention of all I met engrossed by one subject, the prevalence of the late epidemic. The violence with which it had assailed the more densely populated quarters of the town had long since subsided; but it had gradually spread itself, in a milder form, through the whole city.

As I approached my aunt's dwelling my heart sank with a foreboding of evil. A single glance was sufficient to confirm my fears. The shutters were closed: some scattered remains of straw still lay upon the street, though the sounds it was meant to deaden could no more trouble the tired ear of restless fever; the knocker, muffled with the same anxious care, might now sound its loudest peal unheard by the dulled sense which could never again be startled by its echo.

I waited some time before the door was opened. At last the housekeeper made her appearance. The moment she recognised me she placed her finger on her lip in token of silence, and with a noiseless step led me into her own room.

Poor Dorothea was indeed no more! I further learnt that the moment her disorder had taken a fatal turn, the house had been beset by a brood of harpies, who, under the mask of religion, had wormed themselves into her confidence; and finding her possessed of some little property, had left no means untried to induce her to sign a will by which the whole was delivered into their care, to be distributed in charity, or otherwise made over to the religious society of which they had prevailed on her to become a member.

The prime movers of this conspiracy, who had been appointed executors of the bequest, were at this very moment in the house, and in the act of opening the will. I would willingly have avoided meeting them; but I could not resist the desire I felt at once to look upon the mortal remains of one with whom I had spent so many years; and it was impossible to reach the room in which she lay without first passing through that where they were thus occupied. No worldly consideration, however, would I allow to mingle with my real sorrow for the departed; and softened down as her faults were now by death and the near grave, and chastened and subdued as my own heart was by many and severe trials, the memory of every past kindness came over me with redoubled force; and, while I yearned for her voice once more, I felt that I had never loved her living as now I loved her in death.

I passed into the ante-room : there stood the vultures who had preyed upon her. One with a sanctified face, and solemn, snuffling voice, read aloud the injunctions contained in the will; while the rest crowded round, overlooking the document with suspicious eyes, that twinkled with an expression of eager avarice as they gathered the welcome intelligence that all was right, and that the deed they had planned and framed in the name of Charity was safe within their fraudulent grasp.

Startled by my presence, they would have

approached and offered some commonplace words of greeting and condolence; but I was already half-way across the room, and, waving them back from that place of death whose sacredness was contaminated by their near presence, I entered the shadowy chamber, and, kneeling beside the sculptured form, kissed those cold lips. As I remained thus bowed over the dead, I heard the occupants of the outer room steal away one by one, as if conscience-stricken; and then, at last, the prayer I could not have uttered while they lingered near, broke from my lips; and, sobbing in a sudden transport of grief, I buried my face in the pillow of my last friend.

I was aroused by the gentle force of some one withdrawing me from the side of the corpse; and, looking up, I recognised Francis!

At another time his presence would have surprised me; but nothing now seemed strange in my bewildering destiny. How he came there was soon explained. Having heard by the merest chance of Dorothea's death, and knowing that I had no refuge but in the home she afforded me, he had felt himself bound, by a promise made long ago, to protect and shelter one who had no other support in the wide world.

We met as those who have truly loved and been separated must ever meet—in tenderness and joy. However our relations in regard to each other might be ordered, however that love which we had once borne for each other might be thwarted or turned aside by circumstances, still, through all, there was a deep under-current of truthful affection which no fate could divert from its source. For a time no feeling was present to either but the one that we had loved, been parted, and had met again.

But no sooner was the immediate pressure of the death-bed scene removed from our hearts, and the joy of our meeting somewhat subdued, than a marked change was observable in Francis's manner. He listened for the most part with deep attention to the account I gave him of such few events in my past life as I could bring myself to speak of: but I could see that at times his thoughts were busy upon other subjects. There was a restlessness in his eye which recalled to my mind our last meeting beneath the portico. His features wore the same unsettled, wandering expression they wore then. I saw that his mind was ill at ease; and what added to my grief, was my inability to comfort him: he seemed melted by my tenderness, while he shrank from my sympathy.

At length, after a pause, during which he seemed by a great effort to prepare himself to make some important communication, he said abruptly: "Dora, why did you not write to me?"

What could I answer? It was not for me to write to him, after the circumstances under which we had parted. Was I to tell him that his never having written to me had wounded me deeply for years; that I had thought myself utterly forsaken; and that, while I felt I had no right to expect him to think of me more, his silence had bowed my spirit to the earth?

Alas! a few hurried questions, and a few more hurried replies, served to clear up the mystery that had placed disunion between us, severing our hearts for years. By some fatal chance the letters which Francis had written to me one after another, anxiously entreating for a reply, had never reached me.

The instant he became fully aware of the truth, his despair was complete. With one deep-drawn sigh he buried his face in his hands; while as I gazed upon him in an agony of mind scarcely less than his own, I felt that I had been indulging a vague hope which I had never acknowledged even to myself; and it was with a twofold bitterness that the eternal separation to which we seemed doomed dawned upon me at last.

The momentary struggle over, Francis roused himself so far as to explain to me the position in which he was placed. He gave me a hurried account of all that had befallen him during the last two years. He went back to the time of our parting: and I now first learnt that he had all along been fully aware of the painful history of my birth, and of my father's shame; and that, divining the cause of my refusal to become his wife, he had never ceased to hope that my resolution would in time give way before his persuasions, until, from my silence, and the total disregard with which I seemed to receive his letters, he had at last been led to suspect that my love for him was either originally less strong than he had supposed, or that absence had weakened his influence over me, and that our separation was indeed destined to be eternal.

It was at this juncture that his uncle made known to him a project he had formed, years ago, and to which he now, although with the utmost difficulty, prevailed upon Francis to become a party. This was no other than to form an alliance with the owner of a neighbouring estate, noble but impoverished. Francis was introduced to the Lady Catherine Blount as her intended husband, and a solemn engagement was entered upon.

By the agitated manner in which this relation was made to me, I saw how deep had been the struggle in the breast of my poor Francis. "But, oh! Dora," he said, "what could I do? Bound as I was to my uncle by every tie of gratitude—for, independent of his conduct on the occasion of my father's will, I had no grounds of complaint against him; and having no feasible excuse for thwarting a wish that lay so near his heart; wretched myself—without a desire or a hope for the future—do you, can you wonder that I yielded?"

"I cannot, and I do not, Francis," I replied. "Fulfil your uncle's desire. Be happy in the knowledge that you have acted rightly, justly. We must no more indulge in the communion we have this day shared: you have a solemn promise to fulfil; and I—but think not of me."

"It is of you only that I think," he rejoined quickly. "How often, when this fetter has galled me, for it *does* gall me, have I turned from this beautiful, but haughty girl, to the memory of my noble-hearted, my tender Dora! Do not for a moment deceive yourself; if I am severed from your side I shall never be happy more. There is but one hope left: aid me, for Heaven's sake, aid me to break this chain! Speak but one word, and I am yours again."

"This is madness, Francis; honour, duty, common justice, forbid it. Oh! believe me, dearest Francis, you will be happier, far happier under the consciousness of a duty fulfilled, than were you now to retract."

"And what is to become of you? You have no refuge, no home."

"I must seek one, Francis."

"Among strangers?"

"Yes!—anywhere; it matters little where."

"Never, never, Dora, while I live! The thought that you were groaning under poverty, perhaps oppression, would drive me mad. Oh! Dora, yet, yet relent, before it is too late. Say that you will be my wife, now, at once; only be my wife, and let fate do its worst: you will then have a right to claim safe and honourable protection; and I shall be free—and, oh! how blest!"

Alas! the struggle was almost beyond my strength to bear; but I did bear, and overcame it. Firmly, but with a bursting heart, I once again put from me the cup of joy held out by the hand I loved. We shall see what it availed in the end.

Francis, finding me inexorable, next insisted that I should in some way allow him to provide for my present necessities. This I could not listen to. He, however, devised a plan which, averse as I was to it, he at last, by solemnly vowing that he would not fulfil the engagement to which he was bound unless I consented, prevailed on me to adopt. This was, that I should permit him to apply to Sir Richard Bruce for permission to offer me a refuge, for the present, at Maybrook, his country seat, now vacant by his residence in London.

This was the very last alternative to which I would willingly have submitted; but I felt, —so strongly was it urged—that I could no longer resist without still more deeply wounding the heart now, on the eve of an enforced separation, bound to me more closely than ever.

The permission was soon obtained. Sir Richard, gratified by his nephew's acquiescence in his wishes, would deny him nothing. He even went so far as to write to me himself, offering me a home at Maybrook; adding it as his wish, that I should take up my residence there, not only as the cousin of his nephew, but as his own niece; and also, for reasons which he would not hurt me by expressing, but which I knew too well, suggesting that I should drop the name of Merrick and assume that of Bruce.

The next day was fixed on for my departure; and it now only remained for the hearts which years had tried, and had only bound more firmly together—which had mingled the first tears of youth, and shared its last joys—to take their trembling, fond farewell! As we stood, two desolate beings, on the brink of that fearful gulf which was henceforth to divide us for ever, every word we faltered forth, every thought we breathed, were as the sweet but transient flowers overhanging some mighty torrent, destined soon to sweep away all lovely, living things in its ruthless course; and as we snatched the fleeting joys to our bosoms, the tears with which we dewed them shook their last leaves like the spray of the waters; while, holy and precious as they were even now to our souls, their memory was destined to linger on yet more sweet and more fadeless in after days, when, sullied by the world's breath, all other lovely things had perished or lost their lustre!

PART III.

CHAPTER I.

MAYBROOK.

"Oh! 'tis the heart that magnifies this life,
Making a truth and beauty of its own,
And moss-grown alleys, circumscribing shades,
And gurgling rills, assist her in her work
More efficaciously than realms outspread
As in a map before the adventurer's eye."
WORDSWORTH.

"I thank thee who hath taught
My frail mortality to know itself."
SHAKESPEARE.

THE whole of that night which succeeded to my interview with Francis, my mind was racked by a thousand conflicting doubts and misgivings. I could not quite satisfy myself as to the part I had acted; whether I had really done well, and in accordance with the duty I owed to others in the widest sense of the word; or whether, taking into consideration the peculiar circumstances in which Francis was placed, I should not rather have been justified in refusing to adhere to the strict letter of that duty. This doubt, as will have been seen, had troubled me formerly when the occasion was one far less questionable than the present. As the case now stood, I began seriously to think that in urging Francis to act up to his promise, I was perhaps advocating the fulfilment of one duty at the expense of another. If, as it appeared, he had no love for his intended wife, would it not be a sin more venial to break the vow of betrothal he had made to her, than deliberately to take another and a holier, which he could never hope to keep in the sacred spirit of truth in which such a vow should be kept?

The more I thought, the more did I feel how weak and how failing I was. But the morning dawned; and with it came soberer and more worldly thoughts; and when I recurred to Francis's dependent situation, and the probable consequences of his uncle's displeasure should he refuse to complete the contract, I acknowledged with a sigh that all things were best as they were.

My journey was commenced and continued in no hopeful spirit. As it drew to a close, something of a pleasurable feeling was mingled with other and more painful emotions, as I approached the boundaries of Maybrook. The country through which I passed, hitherto flat and uninteresting, wore a richer and more wooded aspect in the immediate neighbourhood of the noble mansion which I now beheld, its white walls glancing between the double row of stately limes which formed the avenue. Far off a lovely river met the eye, winding away in many a serpent-like curve through smooth green meadows whose undulating slopes, here and there studded over with the oak and the elm, partially hid it in its course, again allowing it to sparkle forth where the mossy sod lay level with its banks. Behind the house stretched a vast extent of woods, now in their full spring beauty, and rich in every varying tint: mingling with the light leaves of the silver-barked birch, towered the dusky larch, while the deep green of the Spanish chestnut was only outvied by the mellower tints of the copper-beech. Far across the park, the deer in groups stood gazing silently with erect heads, or lay basking on the sward, giving to the landscape that last finishing touch which imparted to the whole the soothing aspect of repose.

The whole scene was so rich in beauty, that one to whom such things were new, could scarcely gaze around without experiencing that soul-waking, eye-dimming emotion of gratitude for the bounties of nature, of which no human heart is utterly insensible. But apart from this outward aspect, there was an inner and more breathing life in all I beheld, which sent the tears to my eyes, and gave a trembling pulse to my heart. This spot, so rife with native loveliness, and which was now for a time to become my abode, had nursed the first years and bloomed beneath the dawning eye of my deeply-loved Francis. Here had his childhood worn away; here, too, had his early youth, with all its generous and most holy aspirations, glided on like the gentle stream which flowed murmuring at his feet. Thus when, no longer daring to dwell on what he was, the present was sealed to me, the past unveiled itself to my spirit's eye beneath the magic touch of affectionate fancy; and the tender, shadowy forms it gave me back breathed a charm over every spot, soon to become familiar to me as once it had been familiar to him.

Yet lovely as was the scene, pure and radiant as the dream of childhood of which it breathed, it visited me but as one of those "green spots in the floods" which rise upon the failing vision of some wrecked and sinking struggler with the waves : my joy was the drowner's joy; and I knew that as I sunk deeper and deeper beneath the waters of the world, their phantom forms would vanish and their greenness fade from me.

I was welcomed to Maybrook by a poor relation of its possessor; a woman, meek by nature, and rendered more subdued by her position; a silent, living witness of the effects produced by fallen fortunes and a daily submission to the tempers and caprices of others. She was a perfect shadow. Her slow step made no sound upon the polished floors. The movements of her body bore an exact proportion to those of her mind; the actions of both were deadened — paralysed. Her silvery hair, simply parted on her forehead and almost hidden beneath her cap, gave to her pale face a placid and resigned expression. Her eyes were dim, but not tearful; they wore that look which tells that tears have been present, not shed, but felt inwardly, dropping ever, like caverned waters wearing away the stone. Not as stone was the heart of poor Ruth; but because less hard, the more impressible; and, while she complained not, the silently-falling tears had sunk upon her bosom-chords, jarring their tones. Her voice was the very phantom of sweet sound; the tender, low outbreathing of a heart that knew not its own worth. She was single; yet the jeers which too often assail the solitary woman never struck upon her ear; nor could they have soured her peaceful temper if they had. The appellation she acquired, less on account of her age than of her shielding sheltering love for all around her, was that of "Mother:" and never was there a lovelier impersonation than she presented of every womanly and maternal quality; never breathed there a sweeter strain of the "still, sad music of humanity,"—than trembled along the heart, and melted in the fading eye of "Mother Ruth"—the poor relation!

I learned to love her at once, and fondly. Even now I bless her memory, as a child blesses the memory of a parent; for she gave me more than the world could take away— she gave me hope—she gave me faith. She unfolded to me the pangs, the struggles, the heart-wearing submissions—the forlorn, hopeless aspirations after better things—which had marked the desolate course of her long, cheerless life. She had striven to do well and wisely; but her efforts had ever been turned against her in this world; and as she raised her almost sightless eyes to heaven, she needed not to speak it, for I saw where her strength lay.

The great mistake of my life was at last apparent to me. The sacrifices I had made had not been made in a right spirit. The tree of my life had been blasted, because there was wanting to it the strong fibre of that faith which alone can nourish fruit for heaven; and the lesser virtues were but as the light leaf-veins by which that fruit may indeed be strengthened, but never perfected. Hitherto, I had been dismayed, because, in spite of a wrung heart and a wasted spirit, the end had not answered my worldly hope. I now saw, too late, that, instead of lamenting that all was not well here, I ought rather to have rejoiced, because it would be well hereafter.

Before I turn to that portion of my history which immediately follows, it may be as well to trace out the first few years in the life of one who proved so true and faithful a monitor to me, and to whom I owed the best blessing of my life—that of a spirit set forward in its course, better fitted than it had ever yet been to meet the ills to come. Ruth stands, in the memory of those years, as a connecting link between my then past, and what was at that period my future—now also with the things departed. Her influence over me, gentle as she was, was as great, if not greater than it would have been had her mind been of a more masculine order; a truth to be not lightly passed over, since it serves to show us that the instruments of least power may be as "finely tuned" and to as "fine issues" as those of the greatest. Her opening history, however, as alone it can be imparted to others, will probably convey few or none of the meanings it conveyed to me. It must necessarily be wanting in the forcible colouring given to it by the simple truth of her own personal narration. The world of thought and feeling called up from the heart's depths by each recorded incident, and the tracing out of the hidden connection of each apparently slight circumstance with the sure growth of faith and peace in her soul—all these, with their touching moral, must be sought for in vain. But if a glance at the trials of Ruth Neville bear no other lesson, it must convey one, and a stern one. Let the oppressors of the world tremble to contemplate the possible reverse of such trials in their effect upon the oppressed. Let them remember that the mind which rose up more pure and more bright from the pressure of injustice and tyranny, *might* have sunk down, blighted and soiled, a reckless and erring victim, instead of a sainted one; and let the consciences of such whisper to them with a soft still voice, as if it breathed up from their own bed of death—" How shall it be with me if such has been *my* work?"

CHAPTER II.

THE POOR RELATION.

" She was a woman of a steady mind,
Tender and deep in her excess of love,
Not speaking much,—pleased rather with the joy
Of her own thoughts : by some especial care
Her temper had been framed, as if to make
A being, who by adding love to peace,
Might live on earth a life of happiness.

" Needs must it have been
A sore heart-wasting !"

WORDSWORTH.

BORN to a station she was well fitted to grace, but without the fortune which could alone give her that position in society which was hers by right, Ruth Neville, the daughter of a poor clergyman, distantly related to the owner of Maybrook, was early left, by the death of her father, a struggler for bread, and the sole stay and last support of a widowed mother, and a sister some years older than herself. The mother, with a mind originally not strong and rendered less so by enfeebled health and depressing circumstances, was worse than helpless to herself and others; while in her sister, Ruth beheld an object which called no less upon the exertion of her utmost powers, and upon her loving will to sustain and cherish, than did the parent whose last days were to be comforted or rendered miserable accordingly as she might bear up or falter in the path of those duties which lay visibly before her. A mind like that of Ruth could not fail to feel this deeply, when, their natural protector being suddenly withdrawn, she first looked round for comfort to those who were left, partners in her grief and partakers of her lot; not with that selfish seeking for consolation from the equal sufferers which they have not to give, but with the hope to find in them what she found in herself—the resignation and the will to endure to the utmost the burthen imposed. This would have been her best comfort; but it was denied to her. In her mother, grief gave place to repining; and the spirit thus at war with its Maker failed not to communicate its baleful influence to the other and more helpless of the survivors. Marian, crippled from her birth, and arrived at an age to contrast her own blighted youth—the youth of the deformed—with that of others, the full of life and life's joy, around her, became early soured in temper, captious, petulant, often miserably unjust. All this, in happier days, Ruth had borne unmurmuringly. Her own sweetness of disposition led her to make allowances for the trying temper of her sister, and to combat it solely by the gentlest forbearance—the most soothing tenderness; and for a time she deprived the evil thing of its sting. But, now, new causes lent themselves to the development of poor Marian's mental malady? poverty was added to the other evils which pressed heavily enough before; and her imagination, ever, as it were, probing the wounded places of her heart, made them sorer than before, while it brought no after healing. Towards her mother she put some degree of restraint upon herself, partly from a strong sense of duty, and partly, perhaps, because there were more feelings in common between the crippled in mind and the crippled in body. They, her mother and herself, she felt were fellow-sufferers; while upon her sister she looked as upon one who had no grief, and who suffered no deprivation, compared to theirs. Upon Ruth, therefore, fell the entire weight of the crushed and crushing spirit that could find no other object on which to expend itself. Here first, then, began the trials of her lot, and the struggle of her heart.

Do what she would, it was all too little. Her offices of love were unappreciated—unfelt; and when common affection should have spoken at least in the tearful gratitude of the eye, there met her instead the cold or angry glance, sidelong as in the secret consciousness of rancour, or on the lip words of rebuke undeserved. Ruth had been the most beloved of her father, while Marian, from her early helplessness, had called for and found a double portion of her mother's love; for what mother does not clasp the closest and twine the firmest round her heart, the sick, the wrecked, or the perishing? And now that her best friend was gone, Ruth was taunted even with that. The grave itself was not sacred from the malevolence of the living towards the living. If offence was unwittingly given by Ruth, she was told that she had no father now to take her part, right or wrong: alas! it should have been said that he was gone who would have shielded her from wrong. Unhappily for Ruth, the beauty of her soul shone visibly in her face; and when, as often happened, some mission of tenderness would take her to a distant part of the town where they lived, to purchase from her small store of money, now rapidly diminishing, some new delicacy to tempt the sickly appetite of her sister; and when she returned with a quickened step and a more flushed cheek, the bloom of that cheek and the youthful vigour of that step were crimes in the eyes of Marian, though the one owed its heightened flush, and the other its quickened pace to the zeal with which it had served her.

But if Ruth suffered from these things, the wretched Marian suffered as well, and possibly the more keenly of the two. All that was good within her was of the original nature which God gave her; all that was bad, hard, unjust, malicious, was but the consequence of disease, unsubdued in the first instance by such judicious management as might have turned the worst part of the curse aside. Her struggle with herself; her wrestling with the evil spirit that possessed her; her remorse, felt, but unspoken, might be traced by those around her; and it was never lost upon Ruth. She continued to bear with her as she had ever borne, and the better the harder the trial, compassion taking the place of anger, and filling all her being. But the heart would sink, and the pulse tremble, and the soul sicken under the constant chafing of this home misery; and at last the health of Ruth, too, began to fail.

As poverty darkened around them more and more, the mother, although unwilling to part with one on whom they depended alone for such daily ministry as both she and Marian stood in need of, at length threw out a hint that Ruth might serve them more effectually by accepting the situation of governess recently offered to her in the family of a wealthy neighbour, a retired stockbroker. Ruth felt the force of this, for to her the sole management of their affairs had been confided, and she knew well that the small means now left would be insufficient much longer for their support. She had frequently been on the point of suggesting this last resource herself; but still and ever had she shrunk from it; not selfishly, but from a tender fear, for her character was gentle to timidity, too gentle to encounter the stern things that must be "said and done in the world." She feared that such a suggestion originating with herself might sound like a wish to escape; to quit the lowly roof for one where there was wealth; to exchange the sound of the voice which was certain to be raised in harshness, for that of others which might be kind. Yet now that the word was spoken, it had a jarring and unloving sound; and the heart of Ruth throbbed quicker as she listened.

The hour of parting came. It brought its sorrow to each in different degree. The yearning heart of the mother was to endure its first separation from the child that was now felt to have been never loved enough. A knowledge, too, of the world without, into whose sordid places, and by whose cold hearths the cherished one of the father's love was now to be cast, here came in aid of other fears and other misgivings as to the rightness of the decision which had been arrived at, and added to the pang. Though to Ruth herself, in her ignorance of life, the future was seen through a medium less blank and cheerless, even Ruth felt her courage fail her with something more than the mere sorrow of parting. With her there was, unacknowledged to herself, a secret shadowing forth of unknown evil—of sorrow to come, deeper, and wilder, and more cruelly inflicted than any she had yet known. But the evil was undefined, and she was scarcely conscious of more distress than belonged naturally to this first parting from home.

But the one who felt the separation the

most keenly was Marian. To those who look superficially into the human heart, and do not watch the working of its secret springs, this would seem strange and unnatural. Why all at once should love seem to take the place of hate? and why should the smile that had often and often been turned from in anger, suddenly be as a thing to be missed? How was it that the mother could rise up and kiss her child, and bid "God bless her" with a calm voice? How did it happen that Ruth, who had watched over both as if she had no other object in life than to minister to their need, and who had found all her happiness in the circle of their wants and wishes;—how did it happen that even she spoke cheerfully, as if she were to return the next hour; and yet that Marian, who had chided, and taunted, and wronged her, who had spurned her offers of service, and many and many a time uttered such cutting words as sent the quick tears of wounded affection coursing down her poor sister's cheeks;—that Marian should suddenly in a burst of agonising and uncontrollable sorrow, cast herself upon the sheltering bosom of that sister, and weep tears bitterer and more unassuageable than she had poured even over a father's dust? Ask those who have been the aggressors, not the aggrieved, in the blessed region of home : bid them say what they have felt when those they have tortured have suddenly and in sorrow—perhaps to suffer elsewhere, perhaps to die out of the way of more pain—been on the point of withdrawing from their hard grasp ; and they will tell a tale which shall at once open up the source of Marian's penitent tears—her wild grief—her strong, agonising, but unavailing remorse.

The house—home is not the word—into which Ruth was now thrown, formed, indeed, a striking contrast to the one she had just quitted ;—for, on removing from the parsonage-house to make room for the new incumbent, a lodging had been hired having barely the accommodation required for the widow and her family. Here everything was on a large scale, and luxury, if wealth could purchase it, should have reigned here. The house was a large one ; the rooms were large, the very furniture seemed gigantic ; so cold, and stiff, and bare did it stand out from the walls against which it was placed by hands that would have deemed it a sort of sacrilege to displace it from the formal order of its arrangement. Even the portraits on the walls looked larger than life. The fires in the huge grates seemed ever on the point of thawing the freezing atmosphere around them; but the rooms never warmed. One might have imagined that some enchantment had been at work; and that all this show of luxury without its reality, all this exhibition of the waste of wealth without its uses and comforts had been, by way of punishment, suddenly and magically made over to the possession of some miser, who was doomed to inhabit it with all his own old habits of grasping and meanness still about him; making all he looked on, but enjoyed not, a constant source of pain; and imbuing him daily with the feeling that the hoards of a lifetime were being expended against his will, and he no more profited than if he had made his dwelling in a damp cave, with a stone for his pillow, and a crust and water for his food!

And oh, the dwellers within! Poor Ruth! she little knew what she would have to encounter when she set her foot beneath that roof-tree; it must have been the *Upas* that overshadowed it! But it would be idle to recount a series of such petty oppressions as never place the wrongdoers beyond the safe side of the law; over which no court of equity has any jurisdiction; against which there is no appeal. The case was not a singular one; many such dwellings, with just such housemates, extend over the " length and breadth of the land." Again, I would say,—ask the poor governesses how they have fared? Look into the solitary chambers to which they steal away—if indeed there is a spot to which they may steal for the painful task of self-communion—to ponder over the thousand nameless scorns that have fretted and stung them through the day; a day—and one is a picture of all—through which the cheek has burned, and the heart throbbed, and the eye been forbidden the tear that would have been as blessed a relief as the desert spring to the traveller in the parched wastes of Arabia.

To all such nameless indignities poor Ruth was now a victim. In this abode of the vulgar rich, with no fixed position, subjected by the example of the family to the rude insults of the servants, by whom she was regarded in the light of a servant better paid, and for doing less work, than themselves; doomed, when the daily tasks—the best relief the day afforded—were completed, to take a seat in the cheerless drawing-room, farthest from the fire and nearest the door, and there to remain content, not to be talked *to*, but to be talked *at;* in this abode lived, or rather *faded*, the once tenderly nurtured and beloved Ruth, for seven long years unmarked by any change.

At the close of that time the health of her sister began rapidly to decline. Ruth knew that if she were but at her side, her life might possibly be preserved, or at least rendered more endurable, by kindness and watchfulness; but she dared not give up her present situation, yielding as it did a means of support to them all. All she ventured to ask of those in whose service she was wasting the fresh spring of her youth, was permission now and then to visit for a few hours the sick home from which poverty had banished her. This was not refused; but it was curious to mark how the easy conscience was lulled by the prompt concession, afterwards retracted slowly and by degrees. Somehow or other, the time never served for such absences from the duties which belonged of right to the grown-up daughters of Mr. Gabriel Rigdon. The crippled sister might die uncomforted, and the weary-hearted mother gasp out a pained existence in watching alone by the sick-bed; but the music lesson of Miss Priscilla Rigdon *must* go on; the Italian lesson of Miss Anna Maria Rigdon could on no account be curtailed;

and the evening hours must be devoted to instruction in the mysteries of forming a fat poodle with long ears, upon a piece of Berlin canvas, before the frame of which the eldest feminine hope of the Rigdons bent with a brow of intense study, varied in expression only by momentary pauses of contemplative admiration.

And now, when most her soul was tried, bent, and bowed beneath the burthen of existence, and when kindness was most thirsted for, faint glimpses of it found her; not enough to sweeten life, but only by its contrast to make the old taste of bitterness more bitter on the lip.

About this time, a ward of Mr. Rigdon's, a youth of superior birth and education, and secretly destined by his guardian to be more closely connected to the family by a marriage with one of the daughters, having completed a college education, came to stay some time at the house. From him—and it was the first she had known under those uncharitable walls —Ruth received something like kindness. But it brought with it a heavy penalty; for it subjected her to worse trials than she had yet met. In spite of the most guarded conduct on her part, every look and action was now marked, and perverted from its real and simple truth, and openly and insultingly commented upon by those in the path of whose fortunes her beauty seemed to stand. Ruth never could quite comprehend whether she had been beloved or not; or rather, whether any such feeling had existed as would in time have ripened into affection, or whether she had been trifled with. Slight occurrences, unmarked by all but herself, had sometimes led her to think that what she at first took for kindness, was in reality something less genuine—the indulgence of a vanity—the desire to win the affections which, when won, were valueless to the possessor. But such suggestions came slowly to her, for her nature was trustful; and it was not till all was passed that *that* thought —the bitterest of all—had full power to rankle in her breast. Her one feeling at the time was, that love *might* have bloomed for her there, had there been soil and space for its growth. But, if it were so, the tender plant was checked in its early and fresh upspringing, and all that her gentle nature was ever to know of its sweetness was compassed within those few brief months when, in the overflowing gratitude of her heart, her mind awakened and refreshed by sympathy, the dawnings of sweet fancies visited her, and like a dream she seemed to see—to feel—that *one* other spirit, fairer even than those which guarded the old household affections, was winging its bright way across her path; but, alas! doomed neither to flag nor to tarry in its course, but to sweep onward, farther and farther from her house of life, and finally to settle down and fold its wings beside some happier hearth, where the undying hopes might yet be fanned into life, and where the ashes of joy were not all extinguished!

The end was, that Ruth, guileless and devoted as the being whose name she bore,

> " When, sick for home
> She stood in tears amid the alien corn,"

was forced at last to seek refuge in her home; forced, innocent as she was, to slink back like a culprit, and to take her place once again, herself unsupported, beside those who needed support still more.

Thus far the story of Ruth was related to me by herself, except such portions of it as touched upon her sister's conduct to herself, which I gathered from other sources; and so far every, even the most minute circumstance, would be dwelt upon by her as if it were a thing of yesterday. But never beyond the point of that transient love-dream could I induce her to fix her attention closely upon the sad events of her life. A cloud seemed to have settled upon her heart from that hour. Like one who, though but for a moment, had looked intently on the sun, ever afterwards, wherever her eye turned, darkness seemed to rest. From that time life seemed to have lost its interest. She felt subdued in spirit, for she had been chastened; yet she acknowledged that she had been so chastened in love, even the love of a Father. She began thenceforward to live for others, even more entirely than she had hitherto done, if that were possible; and her ministry now was directed more to the soul than to the body. She became a watcher beside death-beds; and, among others, and first, those of her mother and Marian; the one passing away in unconsciousness of all around her—the other in a penitence of heart, at once touching and true. After they were gone from her, she lived all her uncheered life in strange homes, teaching the young; and often going through a repetition of such scenes as had early sickened her of life, and served to raise her hopes higher. Sometimes her lot had been less galling, but that was rarely; and when at last her existence was made known to Sir Richard Bruce, as the last survivor of that branch of his family represented by her father; and when, by his wish, originating partly in pride, partly in compassion, she was transferred for the remainder of her days to Maybrook, she laid down the burthen of life as entirely as if she had found her grave. The power of suffering seemed worn out—dead within her; love, and peace, and gentleness, and piety, and deep faith alone surviving, beautifying the stilly calm of her life's close, which, like that of day, sank down with a crowning halo, its very clouds gilded till darkness became light, and the beams from heaven spreading a tender and a loving radiance over all!

CHAPTER III.

THE LORD OF THE MANOR.

" His name could sadden, and his deeds surprise;
But they that feared him, dared not to despise.
Too high for common selfishness, he could
At times resign his own for others' good,
But not in pity, not because he ought.
But in some strange perversity of thought
That swayed him onward with a secret pride
To do what few, or none, would do beside."
                                        BYRON.

THE time was soon to come when I should need all comfort, all counsel. A few weeks only passed over my head before news arrived of Francis's marriage; and scarcely had my mind in some degree recovered from the bitter consciousness of the utter separation that was between us, when a letter was one day put into my hand, containing the unwelcome intelligence that Sir Richard Bruce was to be expected immediately at Maybrook. His appearance I had determined upon as a signal for my own departure to seek a home elsewhere; his arrival, however, followed so closely upon its announcement, that I found it impossible to take any steps towards the furtherance of my object, until, as will be seen, his coming effectually overthrew my design.

On the day of the expected arrival, there was a hurried show of preparation throughout the beautiful domain of Maybrook, betraying an anxiety to propitiate a hard task-master, rather than to win the good-will of a lenient judge; from which it was evident that Sir Richard Bruce, although justly respected for his many high and noble qualities, his strict principles, his rigid regard for truth, and his deep sense of honour, was yet a man more feared than loved. Ruth alone moved about in her usual quiet way, neither disturbed out of her own placid temper, nor heeding the complaints of others, unless it were to utter some gentle admonition, soothing them into patience by the "soft word" that "turneth away wrath."

Finding that its owner was not likely to reach Maybrook until a late hour, I retired to my room in order to avoid, for that day, at least, a meeting to which I looked forward with no little repugnance. I could not help feeling myself an intruder; and my pride was doubly wounded by the knowledge that, however unoffending myself, I was yet an object of aversion, or, at best, of pity, from the unfortunate circumstance of my birth.

As evening closed in, my nervous apprehension increased ; until at last as the great bell rang out its warning peal, the throbbings of my heart were deepened to painfulness. There was no longer a hope of escape: he I dreaded was under the same roof, and on the morrow I must meet him.

Some hours had elapsed ; and so agitated and unnerved did I feel, that I had not yet thought of retiring for the night, when my door was softly opened, and Ruth made her appearance. She said she feared I might have been disturbed by the noise, and came to ascertain if I was well. From her I learned that the commotion to which she referred was occasioned by the sudden dismissal of the steward. The man's rage had known no bounds, and his violent exclamations of passion had resounded through the house. The cause of this strong measure on the part of his master was known only to the man himself; and the whole affair bore so much the appearance of hasty judgment, if not of harshness, that the terror with which I looked forward to the next day's meeting was augmented in no common degree.

No sooner was the hour of breakfast over, than I received a message from Sir Richard, desiring to see me in his library. Glad to get the interview over, I descended at once, and with a trembling hand opened the door of the room where he awaited me.

He rose at my entrance, and, advancing to meet me, took my hand, while with a smile that lit up his really noble and dignified features, he welcomed me to Maybrook.

My terrors were dissipated at once. I no longer saw before me a being to fear; but rather one towards whom I was bound to indulge no feelings save those of respect and gratitude. As he fixed his eyes upon my face with a searching, but not obtrusive gaze, he seemed to read what was passing in my mind; and as my confidence increased, the kindness with which he received me increased also.

After a few general remarks upon indifferent subjects, he asked me if I had heard anything of what took place on the previous night. On my telling him that I had, "You are probably not aware," he pursued, "how far you were a party concerned in this?"

Without waiting an answer, he proceeded to draw from his escritoire a small packet of letters, sealed, but having no post-mark. Placing these in my hands, he inquired if I recognised the handwriting. Too well did I know it! Too clearly did the truth dawn upon me! Treachery had been at work; and I was at no loss to divine that these were indeed the letters which should have reached me long ago.

Concealing my emotion as well as I could, I replied, "Yes, this is the hand of my cousin Francis; these, I have little doubt, are the letters of which he told me, and which I should have received some time back."

"The letters," he said, "are, as you perceive, unopened. They were placed in my hands last night by my steward, whom I at once dismissed for his treachery. Conceiving, I suppose, that—that—in short, that any correspondence of the kind on the part of my nephew must be unpleasing to me, this man, with a view to advance himself in my favour, intercepted the whole of Francis's letters to you during the period to which they refer. In regard to my opinion on such points," he added, somewhat dryly, "the man was rather under a mistake. However, the affair is, I presume, of little moment; and your better judgment will, I have no doubt, exonerate me from all share in so despicable an act, and do me the justice to believe, that had these papers fallen into my hands earlier, they would immediately have been transmitted to you."

I hastened to assure him of the deep sense I entertained of the honourable manner in which he had acted towards me; expressing, at the same time, my regret that any circumstance in which I was concerned should have led to so much annoyance on his part.

The letters were still in my hand. I hesitated what to do. I longed to look into them —dear as they would once have been to me; but the feelings they would inspire were no longer to be indulged. It pained me to part from them; it was like the rending away of the last tie that had wound itself about my heart. But the strict sense of honour and duty, which I reverenced in the person of him whose eye was upon me, passed into my own breast. I no longer hesitated; but, advancing towards the fire, consigned them one and all to the flames.

I then returned to my seat, and avoiding any further recurrence to a subject so fraught with pain, proceeded to make known the plan I had in view for the future.

No sooner, however, had I alluded to my intention of going out into the world in the capacity of a dependent, than I became aware of the unpleasing impression my communication made upon my auditor. At first he remained silent, merely raising his eyebrows with an expression of wondering astonishment.

"So," he said at last, somewhat abruptly, "you are tired of Maybrook already?"

"Not so," I replied; "happy are they whose fate it is to live and die here; but for me, grateful as I must feel for its shelter at a time when I had no other, pardon me when I say, that for the future I must seek a home elsewhere."

"Pardon me, also," he rejoined with some asperity; "but your project is one most unheard-of and extravagant. Never can I permit it to be said, that one to whom I had offered protection found it necessary to seek it elsewhere, and, above all, in a menial capacity. No," he proceeded, still more warmly, "from this hour I look upon you as my niece, and as one who is bound to uphold the name she bears. Should your residence here prove irksome to you, you have only to say so, and I shall have pleasure in providing you another home, which, however undesirable it may be, shall yet never, with my consent, be exchanged for any place of abode adapted to bring disgrace upon the name of Bruce."

As he uttered the last word, he rose from his seat with a look of hauteur that silenced me at once. But, again taking my hand, in a somewhat softened tone he begged me to consider myself a most welcome guest at Maybrook, as long as my residence there should be agreeable to myself. He then added, that I must excuse him, as he had some important business to transact; and, taking the hint, I thanked him, and withdrew.

Here, then, my fate was fixed. It was no longer in my power to act; my part, henceforth, was to be one of submission.

CHAPTER IV.

DISUNION.

"Take heed: it is
A tender matter to be touched.

Either the league is broke, or near it."
HERBERT.

FOR the space of a year after my first domestication at Maybrook, my life glided on smoothly, but aimlessly. I had much to be grateful for; and my mind, chastened by suffering, and lifted heavenward, no longer repined for the gifts that were denied: in drawing nearer to that good which all may attain, I ceased to strive after the unattainable.

But I was no anchorite. My faith was not one of stale forms and outward observances; it was sufficient to itself—a pervading and abiding principle. Nor were the joys and sorrows of humanity less precious to me than of old. All was calm within me and around me; but the source of feeling was not dried up, nor the fountain of affection sealed.

My peace was destined soon to be disturbed, and my boasted strength proved. For the last few months several communications had passed between Francis and his uncle. Sir Richard had not seen his nephew since his marriage, and had been frequent and urgent in the expression of his desire that the latter should spend some time with his bride at Maybrook. But, to his surprise, and at last displeasure, Francis to every succeeding invitation had returned some insufficient excuse; and it was only at the repeated solicitations of his wife that he at length, with much unwillingness, consented.

The motives which urged Francis to this refusal—unaccountable to others, but no mystery to me—I appreciated and honoured. But in the breast of his wife pride took the alarm; and the disinclination he evinced to welcome her to his paternal home was considered by her as a personal slight; while the restraint observable in Francis's letters, and the wilfulness and caprice exhibited in those of Lady Catharine, left no doubt that the disunion which was to be the result of their marriage had already commenced.

This idea added still more to the painful anticipations with which I awaited their coming. My own sorrow I might bear; but that of Francis how should I support? The woman's heart within me was silenced, but not dead. Could I see his happiness wrecked, and yet be calm? Could I know that his bosom was bleeding, and not say, "This is my work?"

They came at last; but not alone. They were accompanied by Francis's early friend, Willoughby, who had been their guest almost from the time of their marriage—sad evidence of what was passing in that home, the marriage home, when a third was needed to fill the gulf between two beings who stood chained, but apart; miserable slaves! whose groans, stifled but felt along the heart, told of no release but death—no refuge but the grave.

With what mingled emotions I welcomed them, with what strange thronging sensations my mind was filled, may be well supposed, when that fair face which had haunted my dreams amid the night-waves at sea, bloomed before me again; and when in the bosom-friend of Francis I recognised the third figure which had met my view on that night of the theatre!—forms and faces never to be effaced from memory while life lasted; and wherefore? Because, alas, poor woman's heart! they were associated with the object of her one, fond, fruitless, undivided, imperishable love!

But there was another meeting which tried me more than all. I had to welcome almost as a stranger the one whom I had loved more than all the wide world contained. Who has not known some such moment? Who has not felt that gasping of the heart—that after-failing and dying-away of the powers of life, under the strong necessity of concealment, the bounden duty of suppressing all expression of even their best and holiest affections?

As Francis approached and took my offered hand, for one instant, no more, his eye met mine. Alas! what did I read there? Misery, utter misery. There were no bounds to it: there was not the smallest ray of hope breaking in upon the broad, blank shadow of the despair which had settled upon his soul. I saw it, and my heart sank. What availed now the calmness in which I had prided? There are relapses in the mind's sickness as well as in that of the body. My new-found strength was but the temporary scarring over: the pain I endured was the outbreaking of an old wound.

And now I became a grieved but helpless witness of the wretchedness which this marriage had entailed. Yet the chain hung lightly upon her—the wife. Oh, what a stain she cast upon that most sacred name! She appeared to be utterly heartless herself; yet exacting from others the appearance at least of that devotion whose reality she had the soul neither to feel nor comprehend. Weak and vain, with the perversity natural to her, she resented that coldness on the part of Francis which her tenderness should have melted away, and which, while it wounded not one better feeling in her breast, aroused there every revengeful and unwomanly passion.

But there was one part of her conduct which pained me more than all this, hateful as it was, and that was the peculiar levity of her manner towards Willoughby.

Time rolled on, and the house continued a divided one; Francis and his uncle, with Ruth and myself, forming one party, from which Lady Catharine separated herself almost wholly, passing her time either alone, or attended by Willoughby.

And here a new source of uneasiness was presented to Francis. Willoughby had been from his earliest years his most attached friend.

Hitherto they had shared the confidence of brothers; the dissimilarity of their characters— than which no two could be more totally opposed—serving only to unite them the more strongly. But now, for the first time, their friendship underwent a change. Willoughby, light-hearted, and equally light-headed, following the bent of his own inclination, infatuated by her beauty, and perhaps entangled by the web of coquetry she was weaving around him, invariably took the part of the wife at the expense of that consideration which was due to the husband.

But the cloud which was deepening over us, and which was soon to burst upon our heads in storm and terror, is a thing I would gladly pass over as rapidly as may be.

Evening had succeeded to a day of more than usual restraint. It was summer. Not a breath ruffled the glassy surface of the river, or stirred the light branches of the willows that bathed in its stream, as Ruth and myself, accompanied by Francis, stood silently watching its winding course. We were grave; not sad. In the midst of sorrow, an hour like this, stolen from the weary watches of the day, breathed into our hearts a sweet and holy calm, lightening our pilgrimage while it lasted, and, when no longer present, leaving upon its track those blessed influences which no after-conflict could altogether annul. We never tired of Nature's face. It cheered us like the face of a mother; and her voice was as a mother's voice, soothing us into rest when else the darkness of our little world had scared the sweets of repose from us.

So we stood, and spoke not. But though silent, the thoughts of the three were audible each to the other; and we knew that a bond was between us, an upholding and sustaining bond, by which each was vowed to offer to, and for, those other and dearer, comfort under present trial, and prayer against future ill; prayer, breathed out in the still night when the world was laid at rest, and love alone woke to call down blessings on the loved, and to implore for the strength that was needed, and to ask nothing for self, but all for another, and in the midst of outward wrong and oppression to bow the head in thankfulness that all was well within, in the innocence and peace of the spirit.

We knew not wherefore, but we were this night one and all more grave than usual, more silent, more subdued to the hour. It was as if the pressure of some coming ill weighed upon our hearts. The shadows were deepening round us, yet we lingered. It was so hard to quit this sweet outer world for an inner life all bitterness;—so hard to exchange the gracious silence of nature for the harsh sound of an unloving voice. But night was closing in. We moved on; then returned: went on again; yet lingered.

As we still continued to stand thus, indulging in the ever-new delights of the aspects of nature around us, a mounted servant, who had been despatched to the near town for Lady Catharine's usual supply of idle reading in the form of the newest and most worthless French novel of the day, was on the point of passing us in hot haste to deliver his precious burthen at the house.

With a sudden burst of impatience, quite new to him, Francis, muttering some words about "those pernicious novels," called to the man, and taking the parcel from him, saying that he would look them over and carry them in himself, dismissed Catharine's messenger without further parley.

The act was slight and natural enough, had no premeditation in it, yet, though it clearly did not strike Francis, it did me—and I fancied Ruth, too, looked a little uneasy—that such a proceeding, simple as in truth it was, might bear unhappy fruit, and be possibly construed by Catharine into a deliberate interference with her pleasures, if not as putting a more decided interdict upon her favourite pursuit. The man's appearance without the books, with probably the information volunteered that they were to be "looked over" before reaching her hands, would, I feared, judging by former similar misunderstandings, be, to say the least, unfortunate. The apprehension in my mind was deepened by the fact that Catharine had the whole of that day been more than usually excited and irritable, owing to a slight sprain of the ankle having prevented her attending the military ball fixed for that particular night, and to the enjoyment of which she had long been looking forward.

Alas for the so-called pleasures of this world! That night was destined to have other issues than the inspiring music, the joyous dance, the giddy round and whirl of unsatisfying and evanescent delight.

CHAPTER V.

A DISASTROUS DAY.

" Haply you shall not see me more ; or if,
A mangled shadow."
                                   SHAKESPEARE.

My forebodings proved too real. Scarcely had Ruth and I entered the house, leaving Francis outside pacing up and down the gravel walk before the door, and still busied in exploring the contents of the books, than the disturbance began.

Let me draw a veil over the scene which followed. There is something so undignified, so intensely degrading, in such scenes of family discord—all the more, perhaps, when the cause is slight and insignificant—showing human nature in its poorest and most paltry aspect, that it is best in all such cases to pass them over in miserable humiliation and in silent wonder. It is enough to say that Catharine, at the very first violently resenting the fact of having her books overlooked before passing into her hands, gave way to a still more angry outburst of uncontrolled passion on finding that, thoroughly disgusted with the works in question, which turned out to belong to the very worst class of French fiction, Francis had locked them in the drawer of his writing-table, safely out of her reach.

The explanation, had she been capable of reasoning at the moment, would have been simple: that there had been no intention whatever of depriving her of any innocent pleasure, no intention of even delaying her enjoyment beyond a passing moment, and that the final withholding of the pernicious fruit of baser minds was but the after-result of discovering them to be utterly unfit food for any mind not already degraded down to their own pitiful level. Catharine would hear no excuse. So strong a point did she make of having her own way in this and other matters, as even to go the length of making out of so poor a debate a ground for life-long estrangement, insisting on a separation, if finally opposed.

Seeing how serious an aspect the matter was taking, Francis, whose ideas on the subject of the marriage-tie were rather Catholic than

Protestant, holding its institution in sacramental reverence, "keeping faith unchanged" as in a bond that "could never be lawfully put asunder," at last yielded to his wife's importunity, gave up the books, and with them all ground for contention, subsiding into a silent reserve.

So far all was well, as regarded his wife. But between him and Willoughby, who had taken an active part in the discussion, it was different. A sharp contest of wills between the two had led Willoughby on to the use of expressions towards his friend which rendered all subsequent reconciliation impossible. The words spoken in that evil moment could never be recalled, and would never cease to rankle. Between these two the old ties of boyhood were roughly torn asunder, and never could the two meet in brotherly amity again. So keenly was this truth brought home to them both, that the following morning was finally fixed for the departure of Willoughby from Maybrook.

It is easy to plan the house; but who shall say he will be permitted to build it? Out of slight causes there will sometimes arise issues, little dreamed of, involving eventual happiness or misery, life or death. Such an issue was hanging over us now.

The remainder of that day was passed by Catharine in a state of sullen, ill-disguised discontent. She retired early to her room, bearing with her that treasured heap of worse than worthless fiction. Into its sullying depths she would soon be plunged, satisfying to the utmost her taste for the exciting and demoralising travesties of human life and conduct which was their whole aim and end. Whether or not her husband rightly or wrongly attributed her laxity of conduct and vain aspirations after admiration and adulation from every one around her, to her indulgence in such vitiated tastes, matters little. Probably such tastes were as much in fault as the works which fed the flame of evil; such inward and outward evils act and react on each other, and the end can only be that moral unhealth of the mind which becomes in time as fatal to its best peace as the worst physical plagues are to the ease of the body.

Left thus to ourselves, Ruth, Francis, and I settled down to our old quiet. Sir Richard Bruce had gone to town on some law-business a day or two previously. Willoughby was dining out. In entire accord with each other we passed the remainder of the evening in reading, working, and conversing on topics interesting alike to us all, and calculated to lead us insensibly away from the contemplation of home trouble into the higher regions of thought, with poetry and science for our guides. On the table before us were spread Shakespeare and Spenser, Herbert and Wordsworth, with Herschel, Newton, and La Place: a banquet rich in delight, and breeding no distempered humours, but serving rather to quicken the faculties and enliven the soul. With such gales to speed their flight, the hours could scarcely flag with drooping wings.

So occupied, we were none of us aware how far we had been beguiled into the night hours, until we were roused by Willoughby's return. He went straight to his room. Soon afterwards I myself retired for the night. But still the others remained up; Mother Ruth knitting on, and Francis continuing to read aloud to her, till long after the rest of the household had become buried in sleep.

Fortunate indeed was it that this was so. Terrible as were the events of that night, other and more dire calamities might have fallen on that small household had there not been wakeful eyes to watch over those that slept, heedful hearts full of devices of ready help in the service of the thoughtless and unheeding, tender souls alive to the needs alike of the evil and the good.

It seemed to me, as well as I can now remember, after so long an interval of time, that I could scarcely have fallen into the depths of a first sound sleep when I was awakened by the gentle touch of a familiar hand. At my bedside stood Mother Ruth, calm and serene as ever. A whispered, but not flurried intimation that I had better at once rise and get myself dressed, told me without need of further words that some alarm of fire must have brought her to my side.

I did as I was bid, asking few questions beyond a hurried—"Is it much? Are all safe?" Whether from Mother Ruth's untroubled look, or whatever cause, I do not know; but I did not think of Francis till the very last. My thoughts flew first to Catharine, probably because her passing sprain rendered her more than usually helpless; then to Willoughby, who I knew to be heedless and random in all his ways. In such a peculiar direction of my fears there was indeed a prophetic feeling as to who were to be the principal sufferers from the startling events of the night.

The account given to me by Ruth at a later moment, I had better relate here.

While Francis and herself had still remained up, occupied as already stated in the common sitting-room adjoining the library, they were somewhat startled by hearing a man running rapidly down the avenue towards the house. It proved to be the lodge-keeper. Seeing probably some gleam of light through the laths of the Venetian blind which was drawn down, and concluding that some of the family were still up, he made direct for the window instead of the hall door, at the same time needlessly, and as it turned out most unfortunately, raising a shout of "Fire!"

On Francis raising the window and letting the man in, the information he brought was that fire was issuing from a window on that side of the house, the window above the drawing-room, which was that of Catharine's room.

The miserable truth flashed at once on Francis. Catharine must, as usual, have been indulging in her dangerous habit of reading in bed, had fallen asleep, and set fire to the room. The scream of agony which now burst on his ear was a confirmation of the miserable truth.

Turning quickly to Ruth he said: "You must look to Dora; I must see to the safety of my wife."

With that he passed rapidly up the stairs.

He had scarcely crossed the room, when Ruth heard a loud crash of glass. This was followed a moment after by the fall of a heavy body from a window above. The lodge-keeper rushed out, reporting to Ruth that a man had fallen, or had leaped, from the sleeping-room above the library. That room was Willoughby's.

Ruth had waited to hear no more, but had hastened to call up the men-servants, and send them, some to the assistance of the lodge-keeper in lifting up the fallen man, and others to the aid of Francis; next, she had roused the women; last, she had come to me, with her word of gentle warning.

All was soon dire confusion in the house; the servants hurrying to and fro, wild with terror, and scarcely available, with one or two notable exceptions, for any service of help required of them where help was most urgently called for.

Passing from my room as soon as I possibly could, and following in the footsteps of Ruth, who had left me to ascertain what assistance she could render, the first objects that presented themselves to me were the lodge-keeper and another of the men bearing between them the body of Willoughby, who appeared stunned, if not seriously injured, and who was covered with blood. Heated with wine, as we afterwards learnt, he had on his return from the dinner-party of that night, been startled out of his first heavy sleep by the lodge-keeper's cry of "Fire." Making his way to the window, dazed in mind and but half-awake, and seeing flames issuing from a room on the same floor, he had been seized with a sudden panic, and with the quick instinct of self-preservation, regardless of the equal peril of those whose hospitalities he shared, had at once leaped to the ground.

Catharine I found already removed to a distant part of the house, screaming with intolerable pain, and under the care of Mother Ruth and two of the women. Poor Catharine! She had paid dearly indeed for her pastime. Severely burnt in various parts of her body, it was on her face that the fire had wreaked its worst fury; that lovely face, never again to charm by its surpassing beauty, or raise the unconscious belief in a nature fair and sweet as that outward impress of the Maker's hand.

A Disastrous Day.

What a wreck she was! Of her ultimate recovery, or even of the state in which she would be left if the injuries were survived, we could know nothing yet. Medical aid, though instantly summoned, could not reach us for some time. Meanwhile we did what we could. From among Mother Ruth's abundant stores kept in readiness for emergencies, was a large supply of the fine, white cotton wool best calculated to keep the air from coming in contact with the burnt surfaces. In this we swathed the miserable sufferer, and then awaited with no little impatience the doctor's arrival.

Willoughby was even in more urgent need of surgical aid than his fellow-victim, for whom little more could for the present be done. Besides the severe gash across the arm, from which he had bled profusely, there seemed to be present some more serious injury to one side, a leg broken or fractured, as he could not bear the limb on that side to be touched, and continued to writhe under the most excruciating torture.

Of the fire itself little need be said. The forethought of Sir Richard Bruce years ago had amply provided the house with such resources as were readily applicable in cases of the kind. Francis, assisted by those among the servants who had preserved their presence of mind throughout, soon succeeded in getting the flames under control; and though the damage done was necessarily great, it was confined within a comparatively small area. So Maybrook at least was saved.

CHAPTER VI.

PARTING SCENES.

*" Partings, such as press
The life from out young hearts."*
BYRON.

ALTHOUGH the medical opinion expressed as to the extent of the injuries sustained by the two miserable sufferers, towards the amelioration of whose condition our best energies were now directed, had been in some degree anticipated by all, we yet felt keenly the blow of such an authoritatively pronounced verdict as was imparted to us, and which more than confirmed our worst fears.

With regard to Catharine, the mere surface injuries caused by the burns, though they would probably entail upon her disfigurement for life, were yet considered to be in themselves the least grave part of the mischief likely to ensue. The shock to the nervous system had been so great, that any ultimate recovery from it was regarded with serious misgiving.

In the other case, the result was likely to be sad enough. The injuries sustained by Willoughby, though not tending to shorten life, were calculated to make it a burden, by entailing incurable lameness. Besides the severe gash he had received from the broken glass, extending the whole length of the forearm, there was the more important and grievous mischief of an extensive and complicated injury to the hip-joint.

Of the two, Catharine, we thought, bore her bitter share of the calamities of that sad night the best. Hers was a stronger nature than Willoughby's, with larger capacities for good or evil; and, with a better early training, which might have directed her powers towards higher aspirations, would doubtless have proved capable of looking on life from a loftier stand-point. But Willoughby, as far as it could be given to us to judge him under a similar trial, seemed to be a mere incarnation of self. Catharine was at least grateful for such tender offices as we were all alike eager to administer towards what little alleviation was possible under the bodily torture she endured. Willoughby, on the contrary, grew obstinately morose. His natural gaiety of temperament, never hitherto inclining him to morbid fears, or indeed to any serious thought whatever, having relation either to this world or the next, at once gave way, breaking down before a threatened calamity of such fearful weight as a life-long decrepitude. From the very first, he refused to allow Francis to attend upon him. Francis, it is true, was scarcely fit for the office he would so willingly have undertaken, to smooth the bed of pain on which his early friend was so unexpectedly cast, for he was himself rather seriously burnt about the hands from his strenuous and successful efforts first to rescue his wife, and afterwards to extinguish the fire. But this was not the affectionate plea on which such offered services were refused; for the fact that Francis, too, was partially injured had been carefully kept from the knowledge of his friend.

It was altogether a dreary scene of needlessly-inflicted bodily pain and mental suffering. Neither case allowed of much renewed hope. Catharine, as time went on, though healed of the mere surface wounds, remained long in a most critical condition, every nerve of her body quivering, and with a mind restless and agitated. Francis, though unceasing in his care and unstinting in tenderness to the poor sufferer, all whose errors were forgotten now, was, equally with ourselves, Ruth and I, totally unable to raise her up from the dangerous condition into which she was rapidly sinking. We could but look sorrowfully on the ruin before us, slowly crumbling to its fall.

Meanwhile, Willoughby was slowly progressing towards his recovery, if such it could be termed. Although still lame, as it was but too probable he was destined to continue for life, he was at length in a condition to be removed. This was his one most urgent desire. It was, indeed, his impatient longing to place miles between him and Maybrook, which had all along fevered him, and retarded his recovery. Even now, but for this fact, he would scarcely for some time yet have won the permission of his medical attendant to quit the house.

As the day drew near which was fixed for his departure, we all looked forward with feelings of discomfort and apprehension to the parting scene. But like most anticipated troubles, this passed over in an unexpected manner, the pain arising out of the event being reserved for one alone; and on him it fell most acutely.

Early on that morning when Willoughby was to leave us, a note was sent by him to Francis. It contained but a few cold and cutting words, merely saying that under the circumstances which had led to his departure, he must beg to be excused all parting scenes, and be allowed to take his departure with as little *fuss* as possible.

It was certainly best so, on all accounts. And yet, even in spite of the relief it afforded from much that would have been painful, so strange, so cold a farewell, fell like a blow upon Francis. Never had I seen him so restless, so disturbed, so unlike himself as he was that morning. However much he might have considered it advisable that Willoughby should go, still he could not bear the thought of a final separation from the friend of all his life, without looking on his face once more, and taking his hand in the dear brotherhood of old. And when at last the sound of wheels was heard, and he knew that a few moments more would place an irrevocable barrier between them—poor Francis! he withdrew from the window, and buried his face in his hands. So he remained, till all was over, and the sound of the horse's feet grew fainter and fainter in the distance—echoed and died away. It was the last sound that should ever interpret of one to the ear of the other. They never met again.

Another parting scene was yet to come. That too came in the solemn silence which perhaps befits such severance.

The autumn days had drawn to their close, and Christmas, ever till now a time of rejoicing at Maybrook, had come upon us. Sir Richard Bruce, Francis, and I had started for the early morning service in the old bannered church, leaving Catharine to the watchful care of Mother Ruth.

As I passed up the aisle, a feeling of more than usual oppression came upon me, for which I could assign no reasonable cause. The hymn was sung, the service went on; but still my thoughts wandered. I strove to fix them on the solemn promise of pardon and peace held out to all. But the words fell idly on my ear. I raised my head, and tried to rivet my eyes on the speaker. But they were filled with tears, and every object swam indistinctly before me.

The church was richly decorated with holly. Its crimson fruit gleamed over the lofty walls and hung about the fretted windows, darkening in the shade of the worn marble tomb, or brightening above the mural cenotaph of the dead who reposed far away. Here and there the flower of some pale alabaster wreath received the stray berries that had dropped from their boughs, gleaming, to my distorted vision, like the white and blood-spotted tomb beheld in my dream long ago, far away amidst the roar of the waters.

I was suddenly roused by the sound of a hurried whisper near the church door, and in a moment after a quick step passed up the aisle. The preacher stopped, and every eye was turned on the intruder.

There was an ill-omened expression on the man's face. He advanced straight to the spot where Francis sat, and, bending towards him, whispered in his ear.

Francis rose, and went out. Before reaching the door, however, he turned back, and looking towards the place where he had left me, motioned to me to follow him. I did so, and we found ourselves in the open air.

"Dora," he said in an agitated voice, "come with me; you may be of use. Something has happened. Prepare yourself to find Catharine worse—dangerously ill."

"What has happened, Francis?" I asked breathlessly.

"I cannot tell you," he answered, "it would

shock you. And yet it is best, perhaps, that you should know at once. She has had a fit of some kind, and in her struggles has broken a bloodvessel."

I made a sudden stop, and put my hand to my forehead. I felt giddy, and could have dropped.

Francis now repented having told me. "Why, why," he cried, "did I shock you with this? Remain here; I cannot stay; I must leave you."

"No, no," I cried, "take me with you. I must go. I am myself again now."

We continued to walk at a rapid pace, terror lending wings to our feet; for we feared that before we could reach the unhappy sufferer, all would be over.

On reaching the house, we found our worst fears confirmed.

"Have you courage to follow me?" asked Francis.

I begged to be allowed to do so; and together we took our way to Catharine's bedside.

The room was darkened; the curtains closed round the bed. I drew them aside, and almost recoiled as I looked upon the figure before me. Could this indeed be all that remained of beauty, and youth, and pride, and gladness?

She lay perfectly motionless. Her eyes were closed; and their lids, distended and blistered by the tears which the agony of pain had wrung from her, seemed to press heavily and painfully upon the swoln cheek. Her whole appearance bespoke that torpor which succeeds to bodily anguish when the powers of life have been strained to their utmost, and can bear no more.

We all watched her through that night. It was her last. Her breathing came thick and laboured. Feebler and feebler grew the failing pulse; till, as hour passed after hour, we hushed the beatings of our hearts to listen. Once she unclosed her eyes. We bent towards her. They closed again. She moved uneasily. The drooping lid stirred once more —trembled slightly—and unclosed. She tried to rise. We placed our hands beneath her, and raised her up. Francis leant over her. She turned her head towards him—but there was no recognition. There was a sudden brightening of the eye—a glaring, unnatural light, and an attempt to speak. But the light vanished, and the words died away. A moment more, and the head sank back: there was a slight quiver, and all was over. She was dead.

CHAPTER VII.

ROME.

"In spite of all,
Some form of beauty moves away the pall
From our dark spirits."
KEATS.

"Give thy mind sea-room; keep it wide of earth;
Weigh anchor, spread thy sails, call every wind,
Eye thy great Pole-star—make the Land of Life."
YOUNG.

THERE was a solemn pomp and grandeur about the funeral procession which conveyed to her last home the lamentable wreck of youth and beauty: plume waved over plume, and velvet and silver did their best to adorn the relics and emblazon the name of the departed to the eyes of men; while already the list of her virtues, traced in marble, grew beneath the hands of the graver. But in the startling truth, the bare reality of her life and death, there was that which offered a pitiful comment on the world's greatness. Poverty goes without pall or device to an ungarnished sepulchre: the peasant's and the pauper's coffin is an unadorned thing; and the worth which lies hidden beneath the blank boards is left to the simple chronicle of the household voice, dwindling at last into an old village tale. Vice, too, has its record *there:* with the lowly it wears no mask. But the little great must carry on to the last the poor farce of this world's mockeries: the worm itself must be richly clothed lest the dust in which it grovels should defile it; and the mourners go smiling away to think what an excellent thing it is to go down to corruption with as fair a name as if they had earned it, content to consign to undistinguished fame the evil and the just, the depraved and the virtuous, the aged who have died unrepenting, and the child that has known no sin.

It was long before the scenes of misery and death we had witnessed were effaced from our minds. Days, weeks, and months rolled on, and still they lay like shadows in our path. It was in vain that we attempted to comprehend why such things had been permitted. We walked darkly; yet we questioned nothing. In earlier life such a seeming preponderance of evil over good might have shaken our faith; but it was not so now. We had suffered, it is true, though innocent; but had not the burthen pressed still more heavily upon those through whom we suffered? We doubted not that it had. Nor would we in the hour of our greatest sorrow have exchanged the relative positions of oppressor and oppressed : bitter as our trial had been, we felt that it was better to endure than to inflict.

But however the mind may for a time be overwhelmed by shocks like these, their effects must wear off: like those of the torpedo, they benumb but do not disable. Life and its precious things are before us, given to be enjoyed, not despised or wasted; and where the blast has swept over the earlier blossoms, doubly welcome is the later fruit which was forbidden to our hope.

Francis, soon after the funeral was over, had set out for new scenes wherewith to raze from his mind the painful impressions which had so recently been forced upon it. His destination had been Rome. What especial phase of thought had led him to make choice of Rome as the refuge of a weary spirit, we did not seek to know. But the choice, as it proved in the end, was an eventful one both for him and for me.

From the time we parted from him, letters

continued to reach us with unfailing constancy, bearing the eagerly-looked-for Roman post-mark. As time went on, these regular missives began to assume, as both his uncle Bruce and I thought, a marked change of tone. Serious, Francis had always been; but his seriousness was now taking the form of a grave and impressive earnestness new to us both. Passages touching on religious points of discussion were of frequent occurrence in his letters. And it soon became evident to us that this sojourn in the ancient stronghold of the great Catholic Faith was telling upon his views and convictions. One expression which he used struck us more particularly. In speaking of his having been present at the celebration of one of the highest festivals of the Roman Catholic Church, he made use of these remarkable words:

"I felt how strangely—and I may say sadly—I stood amongst them, but not of them; a poor miserable *Dissenter*, an apostate from the grand old Faith of my fathers!"

And now, as more and more his correspondence became filled with the overflowings of a spirit earnestly seeking the good it has missed or lost in the hurry and turmoil of life, I began at last to see more clearly than I had hitherto done—though I had always felt myself to be in entire sympathy with the workings of his mind and heart—how the precious seeds that were ultimately destined to take root in so congenial a soil must have been sown long ago, and sown by a mother's hand!

Yes; now for the first time it dawned upon me that in those early days of our meeting, when the mother and son had come together after so cruel and prolonged a separation, the truths of the Christian faith as taught by that mother during the brief space allotted to her, must have been, possibly for the first time in their full completeness, presented to his mind. Looking back on that distant time when I was myself so unthinking and unregenerate, I could not but remember how often and how long those two, that mother and that son, had remained closeted together; engaged, not as we then in our darkness concluded, in the ordinary intercourse and companionship of life, but doubtless, as I now believed, under the new light that was breaking upon me, in deep and solemn questionings on his part, and in earnest admonition born of religious fervour on hers.

Will it not, then, readily be supposed that the new turn which affairs were taking, possessed a deep and vital interest for both Sir Richard Bruce and myself? For myself, I had so entire a reliance on the judgment of Francis, that I felt in a strange new sense that all was indeed well, and more than well. Even though scarcely yet fully conscious how far my own mind had also been set forward long ago, and by a quite different force of circumstances and associations, upon the track it was destined one day to follow up, even as Francis was following it now, already I seemed to catch far and faint glimpses of that Light towards which we were both alike journeying —he somewhat in advance, I treading in his footsteps—that glorious Beacon which has shone undimmed through the ages, " the guide of nations and of humanity," and which shall continue to glow through the world's darkness so long as that world shall exist.

If, however, with regard to myself, the impressions conveyed by the tidings of this new soul-awakening were so fully satisfying, with Sir Richard Bruce their effect was altogether different. Given at no time to any very deep contemplation on points of religious controversy, he was by no means surprised at the near advent of the reception of Francis into the Church of Rome. He was, nevertheless, strongly and determinedly opposed to it. The result was a long and painful interview between us, in which he proposed to me a measure for the withdrawal of Francis from what he called "the scene of his infatuation," home to Maybrook. He questioned me closely as to whether there had not formerly been an attachment between Francis and myself. To this I could make but one answer. When, however, he ventured to intimate to me that a marriage between Francis and myself would probably, by bringing new interests into his life, tend to wean him from his "hallucinations," as he termed the convictions of his nephew, I made at once a firm stand against any such speculations.

Feeling what vital interests were at stake, I could arrive but at one decision. I would listen to no scheme for the recall of one who had suffered so recently and so keenly in these very scenes, and who was at last finding rest and peace, and more, a sublime and divine consolation, amidst the associations called up by the Eternal City. Sir Richard met the rebuff, as was in keeping with so proud a nature, in profound silence, and it was long before our intercourse reverted to its recent and more cordial relations. The event which, after a long interval, once more restored matters to their ordinary footing, was again a letter from Francis.

That letter—I have it before me now!—was all that his uncle could desire. It touched only very remotely on the subject which had latterly so fully engrossed his thoughts, at least, in words. To me, however, who could read between the lines, it bore a deeper and more solemn meaning than lay in the written characters; and I divined, and truly divined, that apart from all other and more tenderly human considerations, my soul's health was the one point which was uppermost in the mind of the writer. The substance of that letter from Francis to his uncle was a proposal similar to that conveyed to me by Sir Richard himself—that I should in time become the wife of Francis. The only difference was that Francis was looking to a more remote period for our union than at all chimed in with the views of his uncle. Francis expressed no present intention of quitting Rome.

CHAPTER VIII.

THE COMMUNION OF SOULS.

" He spoke as one who ne'er might speak again,
And as a dying man to dying men."
BAXTER.

NO sooner had Francis received from me the full assurance of my entire love and devotion to him, and my stedfast hope and wish one day to share my life with him, to bring him forgetfulness of the past and solace for the future, than I found that I had indeed truly discerned the higher aim he had in view. With an instinctive consciousness that to me only could he fully communicate those deeper revelations of faith, which he had himself already accepted, and feeling also that to me, as his now affianced wife, he had a right to impart whatever he thought fit in separate and more intimately confidential correspondence than he could address to another, he began at once to pour upon me the riches of a mind whose power and reach I had hitherto but feebly comprehended.

At first I was wholly overpowered by a strength of expression, a force of eloquence, which made me feel my own restricted power of language a pitiable drawback to any higher interchange of thought. More bitterly than ever in my life did I feel how miserably my mere technical education had been neglected. To venture to argue with him the great problems presented to me, now for the first time in their full force, was like attempting to cross an abounding stream without the stepping-stones needful for safety and assurance. I seemed lost in the flood. But Francis encouraged me, and by slow degrees led me on to ponder over and discuss with him the most vital questions touching the Catholic Belief. He refused to listen for a moment to my pleading a woman's supposed narrow range of thought and general inferiority of intellect.

"That opinion," he said, "is the one moral infidelity in man which lies at the root of half the evil in the world, benumbing the real powers of woman and depressing them down to the level indicated by its own bitter irony: asserting without foundation, and, in so doing, creating what it asserts." To this he added an earnest admonition; "Never," he said, permit yourself to feel lowered and crippled by that insidious and most transparent falsehood."

So animated, and so sustained, my mental vision cleared, and I was enabled to take a firmer and more comprehensive grasp of the subject. Many points were already settled in my mind, having frequently occupied my thoughts in a vague and hopeless way years ago, and needing but this new field of intimate, patient, and loving exposition to be brought home to my intellect and my heart. The salutary effects of confession, the need of intercession, the want of assured pardon and absolution by the fainting spirit bowed down by the weight of sins committed or imagined, the necessity of angelic guardianship and guidance, all these were almost uncontested, and soon became with me accepted facts. Not so, however, did other questions of more vital import. It was only by a lengthy and almost despairing process that I could hope to approach even the outer porch of the great temple of Confirmed Faith : enter within it I feared I never could. But I strove earnestly, and strove long, bitterly grieving over that hardness and imperfection of nature, that shortcoming in myself which I felt convinced alone stood in the way, setting up a barrier impossible for me to pass. Thus, still, though baffled and beaten back, again and again, did we too, wedded already in heart and in soul as fully as if that indissoluble bond of the Church to which we looked had already made us one, continue the contest with unflinching and unabated zeal.

And, apart from all higher questions, with what feelings was I looking forward to the lasting bond which was ultimately to unite me with Francis? That such an announcement of his wishes and intentions for our future as that which reached me from Rome had moved me strongly there was no question. But that the emotions called up were very different from those which would have stirred me years ago is also true. The startling events of the past year had produced a shock, the effects of which had not yet worn off. The flame of suffering might be burnt out, but hope could scarcely yet be expected to rise from its ashes. The old, vain dream of stability as to the things of this life had been roughly broken, and the newly awakened eye was not yet capable of taking in at a glance the real aspect of the world that lay around it. Added to this, there existed in my mind a still lingering doubt as to how far the proposition made by Francis was really in accord with his uncle's wishes, further than as a means of withdrawing him from Rome. Recalling the past, I could not but feel that there had been a time when such an alliance for Francis would not have been contemplated by Sir Richard Bruce in any other light than that of a degradation. The fatal issue of his own most cherished scheme had, it is true, been a severe blow to him; but he was not a man likely to surrender at once the opinions and prejudices of a life. But then, neither was Francis likely to give up a second time all his hopes of happiness out of any considerations of obligation to his uncle. Both, therefore, would probably remain equally steadfast in their several views. For myself, I determined to remain wholly passive in the matter, resigning my fate entirely into the hands of him I loved, not without a grave suspicion that had I done so earlier it might have been better for the peace of both.

Beyond all hope, however, though not without a severe struggle with himself, Sir Richard, struck with the frank and determined action taken by Francis, and touched by the history, now first made known to him, of his nephew's long attachment and repeated rejection, was, I soon found, disposed to yield unconditionally to his wishes.

When, therefore, I learned, as I soon did, that I was to be received in all love and honour as a daughter of the house, I confess to have been deeply and keenly moved. Melted by a generosity which I had so little reason to expect, and fully appreciating the sacrifice of every long-cherished hope to which I now owed my reception as the wife of Francis, I vowed internally to devote myself to the task of softening, as far as I might, the feeling of disappointed pride in the breast of him to whom I should owe the happiness of my future life. His natural coldness of manner repelled me at first; but, by a strict adherence to the plan I had marked out, and a patient waiting for the full thaw of a heart which I had resolved to win, my end was attained; while, as time wore on, and I gained more and more upon his confidence and affection, I saw with deep satisfaction that he began to look with something like real pleasure on the new ties that were about to be formed around him.

The world was growing very bright to mé.

I could now dare to breathe the breath of hope without stint. Meditations more tender and profound than had ever yet visited me were mine. Love I had known, truthful and abiding love; love cherished through years of heart-break, and tenderest when least returned; love which had been my torture and my comfort, my sorrow and my consolation, as long as I could be said to have walked waking upon the earth, for it was the first reality that had dawned upon me as my dream of childhood faded away. But in the affection which I now dared first to indulge; in the love, sacred in the eyes of man and hallowed before God, which was awaking within my woman's soul, there was something almost touched with awe—so profound was it—so holy—so reverential. I seemed about to enter into a new world, and take upon me a new being. I was no longer to be alone in my hopes or my fears, my aspirations or my defeats, my virtues or my failings, my joys or my sorrows. The sweet household bond of faith and reliance; the constant reference of every thought and feeling to another and a dearer; the daily charities of life; forbearance and encouragement; mutual support in well-doing, and mutual pardon under offence;

gratitude for confidence given, and allowance made for its want when withheld; the gracious leading onward of each other, hand in hand, in child-like faith, through the thorny ways of this world, and a meek reliance on that more blessed after-meeting in a distant and a better; these things were henceforward to be added to my lot. And when the time drew near which was to make me indeed a wife, fervently and from my soul did I pray that in the path of those new duties which lay before me I might walk uprightly and justly, fulfilling them each and all lovingly and meekly, with confidence and hope, in spirit and in truth.

CHAPTER IX.
'REST, ON THE CROSS.

" Blest be the Hand Divine which gently laid
My heart at rest."
" Here, on a single plank, thrown safe ashore
I hear the tumult of the distant throng,
Like that of seas remote."
YOUNG.

IT was not to be. While it fared well with the immortal soul, the mortal shrine which held it captive was doomed to crumble to the dust. That long lingering in the Maremma was fatal. The unhealthy season in Rome, always so carefully avoided by those not native to the soil, did its work—under Heaven. The searching blast of the sirocco blowing from the arid regions of Africa was destined to overthrow the dearest hopes of a life. The last letter received from that beloved hand contained with a vague and strangely prophetic, but scarcely conscious, meaning, a transcript of the last words of Gregory VII. indited from the death-place of the Pontiff at Salerno :

"I have loved justice and hated iniquity, and therefore I die in exile."

Exile, did I say? No. They alone are exiled who are exiled not in, but from, Rome. I can say this, I can feel this, now. Years have passed over my head since that fatal day which ushered in the great desolation of my life—or what we mistakenly call life, here, in the flesh. Tears and regrets are alike ended for me. Another life, another state of being was entered upon by me from the moment when the grave closed over all that had made good to me the things of this world. Even as he was Rome's at the last, and to the last, so, by his teaching, am I Rome's now, and Rome's for ever.

Mine was no sudden conversion. Long, too long, indeed, was it before Faith could find me in my darkness: long before the touch of that Ithurial spear was permitted to pierce the thick mail of question and doubt in which I had almost wilfully encased myself. Nothing of fancied conviction, nothing of desired devotion to the Cross of Christ, I was resolved, should be owed to the influence of the affections. Dispassionately or not at all would I accept the truths which otherwise could have no likelihood of a permanent hold on my soul. The ground, if not of my faith in Rome and her teaching, at least of my separation from all dissent, had, it is true, been laid long ago in my early, and perhaps too impatient, want of toleration for my Aunt Dorothea and her narrow views, her cold, lifeless mockeries of religion, which had struck with such a chill into my heart. The path was not difficult nor the road impassable from that surface region of the soul's frost to its inner and deeper central fire of Faith. Even to the unbelieving and the apostate, Rome has a wonder-working attraction. All alike must acknowledge in her the triumph of moral over material forces, and the justice and peace maintained by her amidst the despotism of the dark ages. All the culture, all the enlightenment of the world was hers. The lofty position, the moral greatness attained by the Mediæval Papacy in Europe proves that to have been no vague or impotent dream which prefigured to the mind of Saint Augustin the one grand idea of 'a city of God.'

So, at last, the Good Shepherd found me, and so at last was I gathered to His fold.

And now, before I pass to the last leaf and close the book, let me turn one passing backward glance on my past life and its trials, and then let its comparatively unimportant annals be dismissed at once and for ever.

What is the lesson which the sacrifices of my youth have taught me? The ennobling spirit within us—the germ of all good to come—is it wasted and lost because the coarse soil of this world is not fitted for its culture? No—oh, no! In portraying and passing judgment on the struggles of my past life, struggles earnest but ineffectual, fruitless to redress evil, and ending only in disappointment and weariness, let it not be supposed that I would advocate the suppression of all generous, all exalted feeling, all ennobling effort. God forbid! No; fervently do I still say, Keep pure, keep bright that spirit within you. Cherish it for its uses hereafter; but hope nothing from it here. Even in this world we may meet our reward; but such reward is no necessary condition of the sacrifices we make. By looking forward to an earthly recompense, not only do we lay ourselves open to the bitterness of defeated hope, but we do away with the very essence of martyrdom, which should ask nothing from earth, but all from Heaven.

Here, then, let me close the transcript of my joys and my sorrows; not without a hope that the lesson they enforce may be brought home to the failing in all gentleness and humility, with a voice as a voice from the grave; the voice of one who, however in the beginning of life she may have done unwisely, yet in the end took to her heart the lessons of wisdom: seeking where alone it should be sought; finding where alone it can be found, REST, ON THE CROSS.

THE END.

R. WASHBOURNE, PRINTER, 18 PATERNOSTER ROW.

R. WASHBOURNE'S CATALOGUE OF BOOKS,

18 PATERNOSTER ROW, LONDON.

Any Book in this Catalogue sent free on receipt of P.O. Order payable to Robert Washbourne, at the General Post Office, or half-penny stamps (not penny ones) accepted.

NEW BOOKS.

The Faith of our Fathers: Being a Plain Exposition and Vindication of the Church founded by our Lord Jesus Christ. By Rt. Rev. James Gibbons, D.D., 12mo. 4s.; paper covers, 2s. nett.

"The author is not aggressive; is never bitter, never sneers, nor deals in sarcasm or ridicule; does not treat his reader as a foe to be beaten, but as a brother to be persuaded. His sense of religion is too deep to allow him to make light of any honest faith. We perceive on every page the reverend and Christian bishop who knows that charity and not hate is the divine power of the Church; the fire that sets the world ablaze. It is not necessary that we should say more in commendation of this treatise. It will most certainly have a wide circulation, and its merits will be advertised by every reader. Bishop Gibbons has written chiefly for Protestants, but we hope his book will find entrance into every Catholic family."—*Catholic World.*

The Panegyrics of Fr. Segneri, S.J. Translated from the original Italian. With a preface by the Rev. William Humphrey, S.J. 12mo., 5s.

"Happily eloquence was not the only great excellence of Segneri. His matter is always most valuable, for he was a thorough theologian as well as a wonderful preacher."—*Month.*

The Story of the Life of St. Paul. By M. F. S., author of "Legends of the Saints," &c., &c. 12mo., 2s. 6d.

"That delightful writer for the young, the author of 'Tom's Crucifix,' 'Catherine Hamilton,' 'Stories of the Saints,' 'Stories of Martyr Priests,' and many other works of similar excellence and interest, has found a most attractive theme for her prolific pen in the wonderful and edifying story of S. Paul. The Story of S. Paul thus written will be a favourite with those juvenile Catholic readers who have already so much cause for gratitude to M. F. S."—*Weekly Register.*

My Conversion and Vocation. By Rev. Father Schouvaloff, Barnabite. Translated from the French, with an Appendix by the Rev. Father C. Tondini, Barnabite. 12mo., 5s.

"This is a very edifying and a very readable book. Some books are readable without being precisely edifying, and many works are edifying though not at all readable, but this work has both good qualities. It is an autobiography, the record of the trials, struggles, temptations, doubts, fears, calls to grace, and the final victory of a Russian nobleman. It is founded, perhaps not altogether unconsciously, on one of the greatest works ever produced by a human pen—'The Confessions of S. Augustine.'"—*Tablet.*

Men and Women of the English Reformation from the days of Wolsey to the death of Cranmer. By S. H. Burke, M.A. 2 vols., 12mo., 10s.

"The author produces evidence that cannot be gainsaid."—*Universe.* "Interesting and valuable."—*Tablet.* "A clever and well-written historical statement."—*Month.*

*** *Though this Catalogue does not contain many of the books of other Publishers, R. W. can supply all of them, no matter by whom they are published. All orders, so far as possible, will be executed the same day.*

School Books, Copy Books, and other Stationery, Rosaries, Medals, Crucifixes, Scapulars, Incense, Candlesticks, Vases, and other Church requisites supplied.

Three Sketches of Life in Iceland. By Carl Andersen. Translated by Myfanwy Fenton. Dedicated to H. R. H. the Princess of Wales. 12mo., 2s. 6d.

Fluffy. A Tale for Boys. By M. F. S., author of "Tom's Crucifix, and other Tales." 12mo., 3s. 6d.

"A charming little story. The narrative is as wholesome throughout as a breath of fresh air, and as beautiful in the spirit of it as a beam of moonlight."—*Weekly Register.*

The Feasts of Camelot; with the Tales that were told there. By Eleanora Louisa Hervey. 12mo., 3s. 6d.

"This is really a very charming collection of tales, told, as is evident from the title, by the Knights of the Round Table, at the Court of King Arthur. It is good for children and for grown up people too, to read these stories of knightly courtesy and adventure and of pure and healthy romance, and they have never been written in a more attractive style than by Mrs. Hervey in this little volume."—*Tablet.* "Elegant and imaginative invention, well selected language, and picturesque epithet."—*Athenæum.* "Full of chivalry and knightly deeds, not unmixed with touches of quaint humour."—*Court Journal.* "A graceful and pleasing collection of stories."—*Daily News.* "Quaint and graceful little stories."—*Notes and Queries.* "There is a high purpose in this charming book, one which is steadily pursued—it is the setting forth of the true meaning of chivalry."—*Morning Post.*

Message from the Mother Heart of Mary. 4d. and 6d.

The Eucharistic Year; or, Preparation and Thanksgiving for Holy Communion on all the Sundays and the principal Feasts of the Year. 18mo., 4s.

Life of S. Angela Merici, Foundress of the Ursulines. From the French of the Abbé G. Beetemé. 12mo., 4s. 6d.

Catechism Made Easy. By Rev. H. Gibson. Vol. 3, 12mo., 4s.

A Hundred Years Ago; or, a Narrative of Events leading to the Marriage and Conversion to the Catholic Faith of Mr. and Mrs Sidney, of Cowpen Hall, Northumbrland. By their Grand-daughter. 12mo., 2s. 6d.

The Franciscan Annals and Monthly Bulletin of the Third Order of S. Francis. 8vo., 6d.

The Angelus. A Catholic Monthly Magazine, containing tales and other interesting reading. 8vo., 1d. Volume for 1876, cloth, 2s. 6d.

Vespers and Benediction Service. Composed and harmonized by Leopold de Prins. 4to., 3s. 6d. nett.

Catholic Hymnal. English Words. For Children, Church, Convent, Confraternity and Catholic Family Use. For one, two, or four voices, with accompaniment. By Leopold de Prins. 4to., 2s.; bound, 3s. nett.

Rest, on the Cross. By E. L. Hervey. 12mo., 3s. 6d. *In the press.*

Captain Rougemont; the Miraculous Conversion. 8vo., 2s.

Album of Christian Art. Twenty-three original compositions of Professor Klein, in Vienna. 4to., 6s.

ADELSTAN (Countess), Sketch of her Life and Letters
An abridged translation from the French of the Rev. Père Marquigny, S.J., by E. A. M. 12mo., 1s. and 2s. 6d. *See* page 11.

Adolphus; or, the Good Son. 18mo., 6d.

Adventures of a Protestant in Search of a Religion. By Iota. 12mo., 3s. and 5s.

R. Washbourne, 18 Paternoster Row, London.

AGNEW (Mme.), Convent Prize Book. 12mo., 2s. 6d.; gilt, 3s. 6d.; calf or morocco, 7s. 6d.

A Hundred Years Ago; or, a Narrative of Events leading to the Marriage and Conversion to the Catholic Faith of Mr. and Mrs. Sidney, of Cowpen Hall, Northumberland; to which are added a few other Incidents in their Life. By their Grand-daughter. 12mo., 2s. 6d.

A'KEMPIS—Following of Christ. Pocket Edition, 32mo., 1s.; embossed red edges, 1s. 6d.; roan, 2s.; French morocco, 2s. 6d.; calf or morocco, 4s. 6d.; gilt, 5s. 6d. Also in ivory, with rims and clasp, 15s. and 16s.; morocco antique, with two elegant brass corners and clasps, 17s. 6d.; russia, ditto, ditto, 20s.

——— Imitation of Christ; with Reflections. 32mo., 1s.; Persian calf, 3s. 6d.; Border Edition, 12mo., 3s. 6d.

Albert the Great. See Dixon (Rev. Fr. T. A.).

Album of Christian Art. Twenty-three original compositions of Professor Klein, in Vienna. 4to., 6s.

ALLIES (T. W. Esq.), St. Peter; his Name and his Office. 12mo., 5s.

Alone in the World. By A. M. Stewart. 12mo., 4s. 6d.

Alphabet of Scripture Subjects. On a large sheet, 1s.; coloured, 2s., on a roller, varnished, 4s. 6d.; mounted to fold in a book, 3s. 6d.

ALZOG'S Universal Church History. 8vo., 3 Vols., each 20s.

American Life (Forty Years of). By Dr. Nichols. 12mo., 5s.

AMHERST (Rt. Rev. Dr.), Lenten Thoughts. 18mo., 2s.; red edges, 2s. 6d.

Amulet (The). By Conscience. 12mo., 4s.

ANDERSEN (Carl), Three Sketches of Life in Iceland. Translated by Myfanwy Fenton. Dedicated to H. R. H. the Princess of Wales. 12mo., 2s. 6d.

Angela Merici (S.) Her Life, her Virtues, and her Institute. From the French of the Abbé G. Beetemé. 12mo., 4s. 6d.

Angela's (S.) Manual: a Book of Devout Prayers and Exercises for Female Youth. 2s.; Persian, 3s. 6d.; calf, 4s. 6d.

Angels (The) and the Sacraments. 16mo., 1s.

Angelus (The). A Monthly Magazine. 8vo., 1d. Yearly subscription, post free, 1s. 6d. Volume for 1876, cloth, 2s. 6d.

Anglican Orders. By Canon Williams. 12mo., 3s. 6d.

——— A few Remarks in the form of a Conversation on the recent work by Canon Estcourt. 8vo., 6d.

Anglicanism, Harmony of. See Marshall (T. W. M.).

Anti-Janus. See Robertson (Professor).

Apostleship of Prayer. By Rev. H. Ramière. 12mo., 6s.

AQUINAS (St. Thomas), Summa Summæ. By Dr. O'Mahony. In Latin. 8vo., 2s. 6d.

ARNOLD (Miss M. J.), Personal Recollections of Cardinal Wiseman, with other Memories. 12mo., 2s. 6d.

Ars Rhetorica. Auctore R. P. Martino du Cygne. 12mo., 3s.

Artist of Collingwood. 12mo., 2s.

R. Washbourne, 18 Paternoster Row, London.

Association of Prayers. By Rev. C. Tondini. 12mo., 3d.
Augustine (St.) of Canterbury, Life of. 12mo., 3s. 6d.
Aunt Margaret's Little Neighbours; or, Chats about the Rosary. 12mo., 3s.
BAGSHAWE (Rev. J. B.), Catechism of Christian Doctrine, illustrated with passages from the Holy Scriptures. 12mo., 2s. 6d.
———— **Threshold of the Catholic Church.** A Course of Plain Instructions for those entering her Communion. 12mo., 4s.
BAGSHAWE, (Rt. Rev. Dr.), The Life of our Lord, commemorated in the Mass. 18mo., 6d., bound 1s.; Verses and Hymns separately, 1d., bound 4d.
BAKER (Fr., O.S.B.), The Rule of S. Benedict. From the old English edition of 1638. 12mo., 4s. 6d.
Baker's Boy; or, Life of General Drouot. 18mo., 6d.
BALMES (J. L.), Letters to a Sceptic on Matters of Religion. 12mo., 6s.
BAMPFIELD (Rev. G.), Sir Ælfric and other Tales. 18mo., 6d.; cloth, 1s.; gilt, 1s. 6d.
BARGE (Rev. T.), Occasional Prayers for Festivals. 32mo., 4d. and 6d.; gilt, 1s.
Battista Varani (B.), *see* Veronica (S.). 12mo., 5s.
BAUGHAN (Rosa), Shakespeare. Expurgated edition. 8vo., 6s. The Comedies only, 3s. 6d.
Before the Altar. 32mo., 6d.
BELLECIO (Fr.), Spiritual Exercises of S. Ignatius. Translated by Dr. Hutch. 18mo., 2s.
BELL'S Modern Reader and Speaker. 12mo., 3s. 6d.
Bells of the Sanctuary,—A Daughter of St. Dominick. By Grace Ramsay. 12mo., 1s. and 1s. 6d.; stronger bound, 2s.
Benedict (S.), Abridged Explanation of his Medal. 18mo., 1d.; or 6s. 100.
———— **The Rule of our most Holy Father S. Benedict, Patriarch of Monks.** From the old English edition of 1638. Edited in Latin and English by one of the Benedictine Fathers of St. Michael's, near Hereford. 12mo., 4s. 6d.
Benedictine Breviary. 4 vols., 18mo., Dessain, 1870. 26s. nett; morocco, 42s. nett, and 47s. nett.
Benedictine Missal. Pustet, Folio, 1873. 20s. nett; morocco, 50s. nett, and 60s. nett. Dessain, 4to., 1862, 18s. nett; morocco, 40s. nett, and 50s. nett.
BENNI (Most Rev. C. B.), Tradition of the Syriac Church of Antioch, concerning the Primacy and Prerogatives of S. Peter and of his successors, the Roman Pontiffs. 8vo., 21s.; for 7s. 6d.
Berchmans (Bl. John), New Miracle at Rome, through the intercession of Bl. John Berchmans. 12mo., 2d.
Bernardine (St.) of Siena, Life of. With Portrait. 12mo., 5s.
Bertha; or, the Consequences of a Fault. 8vo., 2s.
Bessy; or, the Fatal Consequence of Telling Lies. 12mo., 1s.; stronger bound, 1s. 6d.; gilt, 2s.

R. Washbourne, 18 Paternoster Row, London.

BESTE (J. R. Digby, Esq.), Catholic Hours. 32mo., 2s.;
 red edges, 2s. 6d.; roan, 3s.; morocco, 6s.
——— Church Hymns. (Latin and English.) 32mo., 6d.
——— Holy Readings. 32mo., 2s., 2s. 6d.; roan, 3s.; mor., 6s.
BESTE (Rev. Fr.), Victories of Rome. 8vo., 1s.
Bible. Douay Version. 12mo., 3s.
Bible (Douai). 18mo., 2s. 6d.; Persian, 5s.; calf or morocco, 7s.;
 gilt, 8s. 6d. 4to., Illustrated, morocco, £5 5s.; superior, £6 6s.
Bible History for the use of Schools. *See* Gilmour (Rev. R.).
Biographical Readings. By A. M. Stewart. 12mo., 4s. 6d.
Blessed Lord. *See* Ribadeneira; Rutter (Rev. H.).
Blessed Virgin, Devotions to. From Ancient Sources. *See*
 Regina Sæculorum. 12mo., 1s. and 3s.
——— Devout Exercise in honour of. From the Psalter
 and Prayers of S. Bonaventure, 32mo., 1s.
——— History of. By Orsini. Translated by Provost Husenbeth.
 Illustrated, 12mo., 3s. 6d.
——— Life of. In verse. By C. E. Tame, Esq. 16mo., 2s.
——— Life of. Proposed as a model to Christian women. 12mo., 1s.
——— in North America, Devotion to. By Rev. X. D.
 Macleod. 8vo., 5s.
——— Veneration of. By Mrs. Stuart Laidlaw. 16mo., 4d.
——— *See* Our Lady, p. 22; Leaflets, p. 16; May, p. 19.
Blessed Virgin's Root in Ephraim. *See* Laing (Rev. Dr.).
Blindness, Cure of, through the Intercession of Our Lady
 and S. Ignatius. 12mo., 2d.
BLOSIUS, Spiritual Works of :—The Rule of the Spiritual
 Life; The Spiritual Mirror; String of Spiritual Jewels. Edited
 by Rev. Fr. Bowden. 12mo., 3s. 6d.; red edges, 4s.
Blue Scapular, Origin of. 18mo., 1d.
BLYTH (Rev. Fr.), Devout Paraphrase on the Seven
 Penitential Psalms. To which is added "Necessity of Purify-
 ing the Soul," by St. Francis de Sales. 18mo., 1s.; stronger
 bound, 1s. 6d.; red edges, 2s.
BONA (Cardinal), Easy Way to God. Translated by Father
 Collins. 12mo., 3s.
BONAVENTURE (S.), Devout Exercise in honour of
 Our Lady. 32mo., 1s.
——— Life of St. Francis of Assisi. 12mo., 3s. 6d.
Boniface (S.), Life of. By Mrs. Hope. 12mo., 6s.
Book of the Blessed Ones. By Miss Cusack. 12mo., 4s. 6d.
BORROMEO (S. Charles), Rules for a Christian Life.
 18mo., 2d.
BOUDON (Mgr.), Book of Perpetual Adoration. Trans-
 lated by Rev. Dr. Redman. 12mo., 3s.; red edges, 3s. 6d.
BOURKE (Rev. Ulick J.), Easy Lessons: or, Self-Instruc-
 tion in Irish. 12mo., 3s. 6d.
BOWDEN (Rev. Fr. John), Spiritual Works of Louis of
 Blois. 12mo., 3s. 6d.; red edges, 4s.
——— Oratorian Lives of the Saints. (Page 22).

BOWDEN (Mrs.), Lives of the First Religious of the Visitation of Holy Mary. 2 vols., 12mo., 10s.
BOWLES (Emily), Eagle and Dove. Translated from the French of Mdlle. Zénaïde Fleuriot. 12mo., 2s. 6d. and 5s.
BRADBURY (Rev. Fr.), Journey of Sophia and Eulalie to the Palace of True Happiness. 12mo., 1s. 6d.; extra cloth, 3s. 6d.
BRICKLEY'S Standard Table Book. 32mo., ½d.
BRIDGES (Miss), Sir Thomas Maxwell and his Ward. 12mo., 1s. and 2s.
Bridget (S.), Life of, and other Saints of Ireland. 12mo., 1s.
Broken Chain. A Tale. 18mo., 6d.
BROWNE (E. G. K., Esq.), Monastic Legends. 8vo., 6d.
——— Trials of Faith; or the Sufferings of Converts to Catholicity. 18mo., 1s.
BROWNLOW (Rev. W. R. B.), Church of England and its Defenders. 8vo., 1st letter, 6d.; 2nd letter, 1s.
——— "Vitis Mystica"; or, the True Vine : a Treatise on the Passion of our Lord. 18mo., 4s.; red edges, 4s. 6d.
BURDER (Abbot), Confidence in the Mercy of God. By Mgr. Languet. 12mo., 3s.
——— The Consoler; or, Pious Readings addressed to the Sick and all who are afflicted: By Père Lambillotte. 12mo., 4s. 6d.; red ed., 5s.
——— Souls in Purgatory. 32mo., 3d.
——— Novena for the Souls in Purgatory. 32mo., 3d.
Burial of the Dead. For Children and Adults. (Latin and English.) Clear type edition, 32mo., 6d.; roan, 1s. 6d.
Burke (Edmund), Life of. *See* Robertson (Professor).
BURKE (S.H., M.A.), Men and Women of the English Reformation. 12mo., 2 vols., 10s.; Vol. II., 5s.
BURKE (Father), and others, Catholic Sermons. 12mo.,2s.
BUTLER (Alban), Lives of the Saints. 2 vols., 8vo., 28s.; gilt, 34s.; 4 vols., 8vo., 32s.; gilt, 48s.; leather, 64s.
——— One Hundred Pious Reflections. 18mo., 1s.; stronger bound, 2s.
BUTLER (Dr.), Catechisms. 32mo., 1st, ½d.; 18mo., 2nd, 1d.; 3rd, 1½d.
CALIXTE—Life of the Ven. Anna Maria Taigi. Translated by A. V. Smith Sligo. 8vo., 5s.
Callista. Dramatised by Dr. Husenbeth. 12mo., 2s.
Captain Rougemont; or, the Miraculous Conversion. 8vo., 2s.
Cassilda; or, the Moorish Princess of Toledo. 8vo., 2s.
Catechisms—The Catechism of Christian Doctrine. Good large type on superfine paper. 32mo., 1d., or in cloth, 2d.
——— The Catechism of Christian Doctrine. Illustrated with passages from the Holy Scriptures. By the Rev. J. B. Bagshawe. 12mo., 2s. 6d.
——— The Catechism made Easy. By Rev. H. Gibson. 12mo., Vol. I. (out of print); Vol. II, 4s.; Vol. III., 4s.
——— Lessons on Christian Doctrine. 18mo., 1½d.

Catechisms—General Catechism of the Christian Doctrine.
By the Right Rev. Bishop Poirier. 18mo., 9d.
————— By Dr. Butler. 32mo., 1st, ½d.; 18mo., 2nd, 1d.; 3rd, 1½d.
————— By Dr. Doyle. 18mo., 1½d.
————— Fleury's Historical. Complete Edition. 18mo., 1½d.
————— Frassinetti's Dogmatic. 12mo., 3s.
————— of the Council. 12mo., 2d.
Catherine Hamilton. By M. F. S. 12mo., 2s. 6d.; gilt, 3s.
Catherine Grown Older. By M. F. S. 12mo., 2s. 6d.; gilt, 3s.
Catholic Calendar. Yearly. 12mo., 6d.
Catholic Hours. *See* Beste (J. R. Digby).
Catholic Piety. *See* Prayer Books, page 30.
Catholic Sick and Benefit Club. *See* Richardson (Rev. R.).
CHALLONER (Bishop), Grounds of Catholic Doctrine.
Large type edition. 18mo., 4d.
————— Memoirs of Missionary Priests. 8vo., 6s.
————— Think Well on't. 18mo., 2d.; cloth, 6d.
Chances of War. An Irish Tale. By A. Whitelock. 8vo., 5s.
CHARDON (Abbe), Memoirs of a Guardian Angel.
12mo., 4s.
Chats about the Rosary. *See* Aunt Margaret's Little Neighbours.
CHAUGY (Mother Frances Magdalen de), Lives of the
First Religious of the Visitation. With Two Photographic
Portraits. 2 vols., 12mo., 10s.
Child (The). *See* Dupanloup (Mgr.).
Children of Mary in the World, Association of. 32mo., 1d.
Choir, Catholic, Manual. By C. B. Lyons. 12mo., 1s.
Christian Armed. *See* Passionist Fathers.
CHRISTIAN BROTHERS' Reading Books.
Christian Doctrine, Lessons on. 18mo., 1½d.
Christian, Duties of a. By Ven. de la Salle. 12mo., 2s.
Christian Politeness. By the same Author. 18mo., 1s.
Christian Teacher. By the same Author. 18mo., 1s. 8d.
Christmas Offering. 32mo., 1s. a 100; or 7s. 6d. for 1000.
Christmas (The First) for our dear Little Ones. 15 Illustrations. 4to., 5s.
Chronological Sketches. *See* Murray Lane (H.).
Church Defence. *See* Marshall (T. W. M.).
Church History. By Alzog. 8vo., 3 vols. each 20s.
————— ————— By Darras. 4 vols., 8vo., 48s.
————— ————— Compendium. By Noethen. 12mo., 8s.
————— ————— for Schools. By Noethen. 12mo., 5s. 6d.
Church of England and its Defenders. *See* Brownlow (Rev.).
Cistercian Legends of the XIII. Century. *See* Collins (Fr.).
Cistercian Order: its Mission and Spirit. *See* Collins (Fr.).
Civilization and the See of Rome. *See* Montagu (Lord).
Clare (Sister Mary Cherubini) of S. Francis, Life of. Preface by Lady Herbert. With Portrait. 12mo., 3s. 6d.
Cloister Legends; or, Convents and Monasteries in the Olden
Time. 12mo., 4s.

R. Washbourne, 18 Paternoster Row, London.

COGERY (A.), Third French Course, with Vocabulary. 12mo., 2s.
COLLINS (Rev. Fr.), Cistercian Legends of the XIII. Century. 12mo., 3s.
────── Cistercian Order: its Mission and Spirit. 12mo., 3s. 6d.
────── Easy Way to God. Translated from the Latin of Cardinal Bona. 12mo., 3s.
────── Spiritual Conferences on the Mysteries of Faith and the Interior Life. 12mo., 5s.
COLOMBIERE (Father Claude de la), The Sufferings of Our Lord. Sermons preached in the Chapel Royal, St. James', in the year 1677. Preface by Fr. Doyotte, S.J. 18mo., 1s.; stronger bound, 1s. 6d.; red edges, 2s.
Colombini (B. Giovanni), Life of. By Belcari. Translated from the editions of 1541 and 1832. With Portrait. 12mo., 3s. 6d.
Columbkille, or Columba (S.), Life and Prophecies of. By St. Adamnan. 12mo., 3s. 6d.
Comedy of Convocation in the English Church. Edited by Archdeacon Chasuble. 8vo., 2s. 6d. *See* page 19.
COMERFORD (Rev. P.), Handbook of the Confraternity of the Sacred Heart. 18mo., 3d.
────── Month of May for all the Faithful; or, a Practical Life of the Blessed Virgin. 32mo., 1s.
────── Pleadings of the Sacred Heart. 18mo., 1s.; gilt, 2s.; with the Handbook of the Confraternity, 1s. 6d.
COMPTON (Herbert), Semi-Tropical Trifles. 12mo., boards, 1s.; extra cloth, 2s. 6d.
Conferences. *See* Collins, Lacordaire, Mermillod, Ravignan.
Confession, Auricular. By Rev. Dr. Melia. 18mo., 1s. 6d.
Confession and Holy Communion: Young Catholic's Guide. By Dr. Kenny. 32mo., 4d.; cloth, 6d.; red edges, 9d.; French morocco, 1s. 6d.; calf or morocco, 2s. 6d.
Confidence in God. By Cardinal Manning. 16mo., 1s.
Confidence in the Mercy of God. By Mgr. Languet. Translated by Abbot Burder. 12mo., 3s.
Confirmation, Instructions for the Sacrament of. A very complete book. 18mo., 6d.
CONSCIENCE (Hendrick), The Amulet. 12mo., 4s.
────── Count Hugo, of Graenhove. 12mo., 4s.
────── The Fisherman's Daughter. 12mo., 4s.
────── Happiness of being Rich. 12mo., 4s.
────── Ludovic and Gertrude. 12mo., 4s.
────── The Village Innkeeper. 12mo., 4s.
────── Young Doctor. 12mo., 4s.
Consoler (The). Translated by Abbot Burder. 12mo., 4s. 6d. and 5s.
Consoling Thoughts. *See* Francis of Sales (S.).
Contemplations on the most Holy Sacrament of the Altar. 18mo., 1s. and 2s.; red edges, 2s. 6d.
Continental Fish Cook. By M. J. N. de Frederic. 18mo., 1s.

R. Washbourne, 18 Paternoster Row, London.

Convent Martyr; or, "**Callista.**" By the Rev. Dr. Newman. Dramatised by Rev. Dr. Husenbeth. 12mo., 2s.
Convent Prize Book. By Mme. Agnew. 12mo., 2s. 6d. and 3s. 6d.
Conversion of the Teutonic Race. By Mrs. Hope. 2 vols. 12mo., 10s.
Convocation, Comedy of. By the Author of "The Oxford Undergraduate of Twenty Years Ago." 8vo. 2s. 6d.
Convocation in Crown and Council. *See* Manning (Cardinal).
CORTES (John Donoso), **Essays on Catholicism, Liberalism, and Socialism.** Translated from the Spanish by Rev. W. Macdonald. 12mo., 6s.
Count Hugo of Graenhove. By Conscience. 12mo., 4s.
Crests, The Book of Family. Comprising nearly every bearing and its blazonry, Surnames of Bearers, Dictionary of Mottoes, British and Foreign Orders of Knighthood, Glossary of Terms, and upwards of 4,000 Engravings, Illustrative of Peers, Baronets, and nearly every Family bearing Arms in England, Wales, Scotland, Ireland, and the Colonies, &c. 2 vols., 12mo., 24s.
Crown of Jesus. *See* Prayer Books, page 31.
Crucifixion, The. A large picture for School walls, 2s.
CULPEPPER. An entirely new edition of Brook's Family Herbal 12mo., 3s. 6d.; coloured plates, 5s. 6d.
CUSACK (M. F.):—Sister Mary Francis Clare.
    Book of the Blessed Ones. 12mo., 4s. 6d.
    Devotions for Public and Private Use at the Way of the Cross. Illustrated. 32mo., 1s.; red edges, 1s. 6d.
    Father Mathew, Life of. 12mo., 2s. 6d.
    Ireland, Illustrated History of. 8vo., 12s.
    Ireland, Patriot's History of. 18mo., 2s.
    Jesus and Jerusalem; or, the Way Home. 12mo., 4s. 6d.
    Joseph (S.), Life of. 32mo., 6d.; cloth, 1s.
    Mary O'Hagan, Abbess and Foundress of the Convent of Poor Clares, Kenmare. 8vo., 6s.
    Memorare Mass. 32mo., 2d.
    Ned Rusheen. 12mo., 6s.
    Nun's Advice to her Girls. 12mo., 2s. 6d.
    O'Connell; his Life and Times. 2 vols. 8vo., 18s.
    Patrick (S.), Life of. 8vo., 6s., gilt, 10s.; 32mo., 6d.; cloth, 1s. Illustrated by Doyle (large edition), 4to., 20s.
    Patrick's (S.) Manual. 18mo., 3s. 6d.
    Pilgrim's Way to Heaven. 12mo., 4s. 6d.
    Stations of the Cross, for Public and Private Use. Illustrated. 16mo., 1s.; red edges, 1s. 6d.
    The Liberator; his Public Speeches and Letters. 2 vols. 8vo., 18s.
    Woman's Work in Modern Society. 8vo., 4s. 6d.
Daily Exercises. *See* Prayer Books, page 30.
DALTON (Canon), Sermon on Death of Provost Husenbeth. 8vo., 6d.

DARRAS (Abbe), General History of the Catholic Church. 4 vols., 8vo., 48s.
Daughter (A) of S. Dominick: (Bells of the Sanctuary). By Grace Ramsay. 12mo., 1s. and 1s. 6d.; better bound, 2s.
DEAN (Rev. J. Joy), Devotion to Sacred Heart. 12mo., 3s.
DECHAMPS (Mgr.), The Life of Pleasure. 18mo., 1s. 6d.
Defence of the Roman Church. *See* Gueranger.
DEHAM (Rev. F.) Sacred Heart of Jesus, offered to the Piety of the Young engaged in Study. 32mo., 6d.
Diary of a Confessor of the Faith. 12mo., 1s.
Directorium Asceticum. By Scaramelli. 4 vols., 12mo., 24s.
DIXON (Fr., O.P.) Albert the Great: his Life and Scholastic Labours. From original documents. By Dr. Joachim Sighart. With Photographic Portrait. 8vo.
——— Life of St. Vincent Ferrer. From the French of Rev. Fr. Pradel. With a Photograph. 12mo., 5s.
Dove of the Tabernacle. By Rev. T. H. Kinane. 18mo., 1s. 6d.
DOYLE (Canon, O.S.B.), Life of Gregory Lopez, the Hermit. With a Photographic Portrait. 12mo., 3s. 6d.
DOYLE (Dr.), Catechism. 18mo., 1½d.
DOYOTTE (Rev. Fr., S.J.), Elevations to the Heart of Jesus. 12mo., 3s.
——— Sufferings of Our Lord. *See* Columbiere (Fr.) [2s.
DRAMAS—Convent Martyr; or, "Callista" dramatised. 12mo.,
——— Ernscliff Hall (Girls, 3 Acts). 12mo., 6d.
——— Expiation (Boys, 3 Acts). 12mo., 2s.
——— Filiola (Girls, 4 Acts). 12mo., 6d.
——— He would be a Lord (Boys, 3 Acts), a Comedy. 12mo., 2s.
——— Major John Andre [Historical] (Boys, 5 Acts), 2s.
——— Reverse of the Medal (Girls, 4 Acts). 12mo., 6d.
——— Shandy Maguire (Boys, 5 Acts), a Farce. 12mo., 1s.
——— St. Louis in Chains (Boys, 5 Acts). 12mo., 2s.
——— St. William of York (Boys, 2 Acts). 12mo., 6d.
——— The Duchess Transformed. By W. H. A. (Girls, 1 Act). A Comedy. 12mo., 6d.
——— *See* Shakespeare.
——— Duchess (The), Transformed. A Comedy. By W. H. A. (Girls, 1 Act). 12mo., 6d.
DUMESNIL (Abbe), Recollections of the Reign of Terror. 12mo., 2s. 6d.
DUPANLOUP (Mgr.), Contemporary Prophecies. 8vo., 1s.
——— The Child. Translated by Kate Anderson. 12mo., 3s. 6d.
Dusseldorf Gallery. 357 Engravings. Large 4to. Half-morocco, gilt, £5 5s. nett.
——— 134 Engravings. Large 8vo. Half-morocco, gilt, 42s.
Dusseldorf Society for the Distribution of Good Religious Pictures. Subscription, 8s. 6d. a year. *Catalogue* 3d.
Duties of a Christian. By Ven. de la Salle. 12mo., 2s.
Eagle and Dove. *See* Bowles (Emily).

E. A. M. Countess Adelstan. 12mo., 1s. and 2s. 6d.
— —— Paul Seigneret. 12mo., 6d., 1s., 1s. 6d., 2s.
— —— Regina Sæculorum. 12mo., 1s. and 3s.
———— Rosalie. 12mo., 1s., 1s. 6d., 2s.
Early English Literature. *See* Tame (C.E.).
Easy Way to God. By Cardinal Bona. 12mo., 3s.
Ebba; or, the Supernatural Power of the Blessed Sacrament. *This book is in French.* 12mo., 1s. 6d.; cloth, 2s. 6d.
Edmund (S.) of Canterbury, Life of. From the French of Rev. Fr. Massée, S.J. By George White. 18mo., 1s. & 1s. 6d.
Electricity and Magnetism; an Enquiry into the Nature and Results of. By Amyclanus. Illustrated. 12mo., 6s. 6d.
England (History of). A Catechism. By E. Chapman. 18mo., 1s.
English Religion (The). By Arthur Marshall. 8vo., 1s.
Epistles and Gospels. Good clear type edition, 32mo., 6d.; roan, 1s. 6d.; larger edition, 18mo., French morocco, 2s.
————, Explanation of. By Rev. F. Goffine. Illustrated, 8vo., 7s.
Epistles of S. Paul, Exposition of. *See* MacEvilly (Rt. Rev. Dr.).
Ernscliff Hall. A Drama in Three Acts, for Girls. 12mo., 6d.
Essays on Catholicism. *See* Cortes.
Eucharistic Year; Preparation and Thanksgiving for Holy Communion. 18mo., 4s.
Eucharist (The) and the Christian Life. *See* La Bouillerie.
Europe, Modern, History of. With Preface by Bishop Weathers. 12mo., 5s.; roan, 5s. 6d.; cloth gilt, 6s.
Expiation (The). A Drama in Three Acts, for Boys. 12mo., 2s.
Extemporaneous Speaking. By Rev. T. J. Potter. 12mo., 5s.
Extracts from the Fathers and other Writers of the Church. 12mo., 4s. 6d.
Fairy Tales for Little Children. By Madeleine Howley Meehan. 12mo., 6d.; stronger bound, 1s. and 1s. 6d.; gilt, 2s.
Faith of Our Fathers. *See* Gibbons (Rt. Rev. Dr.).
Fall, Redemption, and Exaltation of Man. 12mo., 1s.
Familiar Instructions on Christian Truths. By a Priest. 12mo. 1. Detraction 4d. 2. Dignity of the Priesthood, 3d 3. Hearing the Word of God, 3d.
Farleyes of Farleye. By Rev. T. J. Potter. 12mo., 2s. 6d.
Father Mathew (Life of). By M. F. Cusack. 12mo., 2s. 6d.
FAVRE (Abbe), Heaven Opened by the Practice of Frequent Confession and Communion. 12mo., 2s.; stronger bound, 3s. 6d.; red edges, 4s.
Feasts (The) of Camelot, with the tales that were told there. By Mrs. T. K. Hervey. 12mo., 3s. 6d.
Festival Tales. By J. F. Waller, Esq. 12mo., 5s.
Filiola. A Drama in Four Acts, for Girls. 12mo., 6d.
First Apostles of Europe. *See* Hope (Mrs.).
First Communion and Confirmation Memorial. Beautifully printed in gold and colours, folio, 1s. each, or 9s. a dozen, nett.
First Religious of the Visitation of Holy Mary, Lives of. With two Photographs. 2 vols., 12mo., 10s.

R. Washbourne, 18 *Paternoster Row, London.*

Fisherman's Daughter. By Conscience. 12mo., 4s.
FLEET (Charles), Tales and Sketches. 8vo., 2s.; stronger bound, 2s. 6d.; gilt, 3s. 6d.
FLEURIOT (Mlle. Zenaide), Eagle and Dove. Translated by Emily Bowles. 12mo., 2s. 6d. and 5s.
FLEURY'S Historical Catechism. Large edition, 12mo., 1½d.
Florence O'Neill. *See* Stewart (Agnes M.).
Flowers of Christian Wisdom. *See* Henry (Lucien).
Fluffy. A Tale for Boys. By M. F. S. 12mo., 3s. 6d.
Following of Christ. *See* A'Kempis.
Foreign Books. *See* R. W.'s Catalogue of Foreign Books.
Foster Sisters. By Agnes M. Stewart. 12mo., 5s.; gilt edges, 6s.
Francis of Assisi (S.) Life of. By S. Bonaventure. Translated by Miss Lockhart. 12mo., 3s. 6d.
FRANCIS OF SALES (S.), Consoling Thoughts. 18mo., 2s.
────── **The Mystical Flora; or, the Christian Life under the Emblem of Saints.** 4to., 8s.
────── **Necessity of Purifying the Soul.** *See* Blyth (Rev. Fr.).
────── **Sweetness of Holy Living.** 18mo., 1s.; levant, 3s.
Franciscan Annals and Monthly Bulletin of the Third Order of St. Francis. 8vo., 6d.
FRANCO (Rev. S.) Devotions to the Sacred Heart. 12mo., 4s.; cheap edition, 2s.
Frank O'Meara; *see* Artist of Collingwood.
FRASSINETTI.—Dogmatic Catechism. 12mo., 3s.
FREDERIC (M. J. N. de), Continental Fish Cook; or, a Few Hints on Maigre Dinners. 18mo., 1s., soiled covers, 6d.
Freemasons, Irish and English, and their Foreign Brothers. 2s.
Garden of the Soul. *See* page 32.
Garden (Little) of the Soul. *See* page 30.
GAYRARD (Mme. Paul) Harmony of the Passion of Our Lord. Compiled from the four Gospels, in Latin and French. 18mo., 1s. 6d.
General Questions in History, &c. *See* Stewart (A. M.)
German (S.), Life of. 12mo., 3s. 6d.
GIBBONS (Rt. Rev. James, D.D.), The Faith of Our Fathers; Being a Plain Exposition and Vindication of the Church Founded by our Lord Jesus Christ. 12mo., 4s. Paper covers, 2s. nett.
GIBSON (Rev. H.), Catechism made Easy. 12mo., Vol. I. (out of print); Vol. II., 4s.; Vol. III., 4s.
GILMOUR (Rev. R.), Bible History for the Use of Schools. Illustrated. 12mo., 2s.
God our Father. By a Father of the Society of Jesus. 12mo., 4s.
GOFFINE (Rev. F.), Explanation of the Epistles and Gospels. Illustrated. 8vo., 7s.
Gold and Alloy in the Devout Life. *See* Monsabré.
Good Thoughts for Priests and People. *See* Noethen.
Gospels, An Exposition of. *See* MacEvilly (Most Rev. Dr.).
Grace before and after Meals. 32mo., 1d.; cloth, 2d.

GRACE RAMSAY. A Daughter of S. Dominick (Bells of the Sanctuary, No. 4). 12mo., 1s.; stronger bound, 1s. 6d. and 2s.

GRACIAN (Fr. Baltasar), Sanctuary Meditations for Priests and Frequent Communicants. Translated from the Spanish by Mariana Monteiro. 12mo., 4s.

GRANT (Bishop), Pastoral on St. Joseph. 32mo., 4d.; cloth, 6d.

Gregorian, or Plain Chant and Modern Music. By the Professor of Music, All Hallows College, Dublin. 8vo., 2s. 6d.

Gregory Lopez, the Hermit, Life of. By Canon Doyle, O.S.B. With a Photographic Portrait. 12mo., 3s. 6d.

Grounds of the Catholic Doctrine. By Bishop Challoner. Large type edition, 18mo., 4d.

Guardian Angel, Memoirs of a. By Abbé Chardon. 12mo., 4s.

GUERANGER (Dom), Defence of the Roman Church against F. Gratry. Translated by Canon Woods. 8vo., 1s. 6d.

Guide to Sacred Eloquence. *See* Passionist Fathers.

HALL (E.), Munster Firesides; or, the Barrys of Beigh. 12mo., 3s. 6d.

Happiness of Being Rich. By Conscience. 12mo., 4s.

Happiness of Heaven. By a Father of the Society of Jesus. 12mo. 4s.

Harmony of Anglicanism. By T. W. Marshall. 8vo., 2s. 6d.

HAY (Bishop), Sincere Christian. 18mo., 2s. 6d.

—— Devout Christian. 18mo., 2s. 6d.

He would be a Lord. A Comedy in 3 Acts. (Boys). 12mo., 2s.

Heaven Opened by the Practice of frequent Confession and Holy Communion. By the Abbé Favre. 12mo., 2s.; stronger bound, 3s. 6d.; red edges, 4s.

HEDLEY (Bishop), Five Sermons—Light of the Holy Spirit in the World. 12mo., 1s.; cloth, 1s. 6d. Separately:— Revelation, Mystery, Dogma and Creeds, Infallibility, 1d. each.

HEIGHAM (John), A Devout Exposition of the Holy Mass. Edited by Austin John Rowley, Priest. 12mo., 4s.

Henri V. (Comte de Chambord). *See* Walsh (W. H.).

HENRY (Lucien), Flowers of Christian Wisdom. 18mo, 2s.; red edges, 2s. 6d.

Herbal, Brook's Family. 12mo., 3s. 6d.; coloured plates, 5s. 6d.

HERBERT (Wallace), My Dream and Verses Miscellaneous. With a frontispiece. 12mo., 5s.

—— The Angels and the Sacraments. 16mo., 1s.

HERGENRÖTHER (Dr.), Anti-Janus. Translated by Professor Robertson. 12mo., 6s.

HERVEY (Eleanora Louisa), My Godmother's Stories from many Lands. 12mo., 3s. 6d.

———— Our Legends and Lives. 12mo., 6s.

———— Rest, on the Cross. 12mo., 3s. 6d.

———— The Feasts of Camelot, with the Tales that were told there. 12mo., 3s. 6d.

HILL (Rev. Fr.), Elements of Philosophy, comprising Logic and General Principles of Metaphysics. 8vo., 6s.

R. Washbourne, 18 *Paternoster Row, London.*

Holy Childhood. A book of simple Prayers and Instructions for very little children. 32mo., 1s.; gilt, 1s. 6d.
Holy Communion. By Hubert Lebon. 12mo., 4s.
Holy Family, Confraternity of. *See* Manning (Card.).
Holy Places: their Sanctity and Authenticity. *See* Philpin.
Holy Readings. *See* Beste (J. R. Digby Esq.).
Homely Discourse: Mary Magdalen. 12mo., 6d.
HOPE (Mrs.), The First Apostles of Europe. Originally published under the title of "The Conversion of the Teutonic Race." 2 vols., 12mo., 10s.
Horace. Literally translated by Smart. 18mo., 2s.
HUGUET (Pere), The Power of S. Joseph. Meditations and Devotions. Translated by Clara Mulholland. 18mo., 1s. 6d.
HUMPHREY (Rev. W., S.J.), The Panegyrics of Fr. Segneri, S.J. Translated from the orignal Italian. With a Preface by the Rev. W. Humphrey, S.J. 12mo., 5s.
HUSENBETH (Rev. Dr.), Convent Martyr. 12mo., 2s.
————— History of the Blessed Virgin. Translated from Orsini. Illustrated. 12mo., 3s. 6d.
————— Life and Sufferings of Our Lord. By Rev. H. Rutter. Illustrated. 12mo., 5s.
————— Life of Mgr. Weedall. 8vo., 1s.
————— Little Office of the Immaculate Conception. In Latin and English. 32mo., 4d.; cloth, 6d.; roan, 1s.; calf or morocco, 2s. 6d.
————— Our Blessed Lady of Lourdes. 18mo., 6d.; with the Novena, 1s.; cloth, 1s. 6d. Novena, separately, 4d.; Litany, 1d.
————— Roman Question. 8vo., 6d.
Husenbeth (Provost), Sermon on his Death. By Very Rev. Canon Dalton. 8vo., 6d.
HUTCH (Rev. W., D.D.), Nano Nangle, her Life and her Labours. 12mo., 7s. 6d.
Hymn Book. 136 Hymns, 32mo., 1d.; cloth, 2d.
Iceland (Three Sketches of Life in). By Carl Andersen. 12mo.
IGNATIUS (S.), Spiritual Exercises. By Fr. Bellecio, S.J. Translated by Dr. Hutch. 18mo., 2s.
Ignatius (S.), Cure of Blindness through the Intercession of Our Lady and S. Ignatius. 12mo., 2d.
Illustrated Manual of Prayers. 32mo., 3d.; cloth, 4d.
Imitation of Christ. *See* A'Kempis.
Immaculate Conception, Definition of. 12mo., 6d.
————— Little Office of. *See* Husenbeth (Rev. Dr.).
————— Little Office of, in Latin and English. Translation approved by the Bp. of Clifton. 32mo., 3d.
Indulgences. *See* Maurel (Rev. F. A.).
Infallibility of the Pope. By the Author of "The Oxford Undergraduate of Twenty Years Ago." 8vo., 1s.
In Suffragiis Sanctorum. Commem. S. Josephi; Commem. S. Georgii. Set of 5 for 4d.
Insula Sanctorum: The Island of Saints. 12mo., 1s.

Insurrection of '98. By Rev. P. F. Kavanagh. 12mo., 2s. 6d.
IOTA. The Adventures of a Protestant in Search of a Religion : being the Story of a late Student of Divinity at Bunyan Baptist College; a Nonconformist Minister, who seceded to the Catholic Church. 12mo., 5s.; cheap edition, 3s.
Ireland (History of). By Miss Cusack. 18mo., 2s. A larger edition, illustrated by Doyle, 8vo., 11s.
Ireland (History of). By T. Young. 18mo., 2s. 6d.
Ireland Ninety Years ago. 12mo., 1s.
Irish Board Reading Books.
Irish Intermediate Education. 12mo., 2s.
Irish Monthly. 8vo. 4 Vols., 7s. 6d. each.
Irish, Self-Instruction in. By Rev. Ulick J. Bourke. 12mo., 3s. 6d.
Italian Revolution (The History of). The History of the Barricades (1796-1849). By Keyes O'Clery, M.P. 8vo., 7s. 6d.
JACOB (W. J., Esq.), Personal Recollections of Rome. 8vo., 6d.
JENKINS (Rev. O. L.) Student's Handbook of British and American Literature. 12mo., 8s.
Jesuits (The), and other Essays. *See* Nevin (Willis, Esq.)
Jesus and Jerusalem ; or, the Way Home. *See* Cusack (Miss).
John of God (S.), Life of. With Photographic Portrait. 12mo., 5s.
Joseph (S.), Life of. By Miss Cusack. 32mo., 6d.; cloth, 1s.
—————— Novena of Meditations in Honour of St. Joseph. 18mo., 1s. 6d.
—————— Novena to, with a Pastoral by the late Bishop Grant. 32mo., 4d.; cloth, 6d.
—————— Power of. *See* Huguet.
—————— *See* Leaflets.
Journey of Sophia and Eulalie to the Palace of True Happiness. From the French by Rev. Fr. Bradbury. 12mo., 1s. 6d.; better bound, 3s. 6d.
KAVANAGH (Rev. P. F.), Insurrection of '98. 12mo., 1s. 6d.
Keighley Hall, and other Tales. By E. King. 18mo., 6d.; cloth, 1s.; stronger bound, 1s. 6d.; gilt, 2s.
KENNY (Dr.), New Year's Gift to our Heavenly Father. 32mo., 4d.
—————— Young Catholic's Guide to Confession and Holy Communion. 32mo., 4d.; cloth, 6d.; red edges, 9d.; roan, 1s. 6d.; calf or morocco, 2s. 6d.
KERNEY (M. T.), Compendium of History. 12mo., 5s.
Key of Heaven. *See* Prayers, page 31.
KINANE (Rev. T. H.), Dove of the Tabernacle. 18mo., 1s. 6d.
KING (Elizabeth), Keighley Hall, and other Tales. 18mo., 6d.; cloth, 1s.; stronger bound, 1s. 6d.; gilt, 2s.
—————— The Silver Teapot. 18mo., 4d.
Knight of the Faith. *See* Laing (Rev. Dr.).

R. Washbourne, 18 *Paternoster Row, London.*

LA BOUILLERIE (Mgr. de), The Eucharist and the Christian Life. Translated by L. C. 12mo., 3s. 6d.

LACORDAIRE'S Conferences. 12mo., God, 6s.; God and Man, 6s.; Jesus Christ, 6s.; Life, 3s. 6d.

Lady Mildred's Housekeeper, A Few Words from. 12mo., 2d.

LAIDLAW (Mrs. Stuart), Letters to my God-child. No. 4. On the Veneration of the Blessed Virgin. 16mo., 4d.

LAING (Rev. Dr,), Blessed Virgin's Root traced in the Tribe of Ephraim. 8vo., 10s. 6d.

———— Descriptive Guide to the Mass. 12mo., 1s. and 1s. 6d.

———— Knight of the Faith. 12mo., 4s.

    Absurd Protestant Opinions concerning *Intention*, and Spelling Book of Christian Philosophy. 4d.
    Catholic, not Roman Catholic. 4d.
    Challenge to the Churches of England, Scotland, and all Protestant Denominations. 1d.
    Favourite Fallacy about Private Judgment and Inquiry. 1d.
    Protestantism against the Natural Moral Law. 1d.
    What is Christianity? 6d.
    Whence does the Monarch get his right to Rule? 2s. 6d.

LAMBILOTTE (Pere), The Consoler. Translated by Abbot Burder. 12mo., 4s. 6d.; red edges, 5s.

LANGUET (Mgr.), Confidence in the Mercy of God. Translated by Abbot Burder. 12mo., 3s.

Last of the Catholic O'Malleys. By M. Taunton. 18mo., 1s. 6d.; stronger bound, 2s.

Leaflets. 1d. each, or 1s. 2d. per 100 post free.

    Act of Consecration to the Sacred Heart. 6s. per 100.
    Act of Reparation to the Sacred Heart.
    Archconfraternity of the Agonising Heart of Jesus and the Compassionate Heart of Mary: Prayers for the Dying.
    Archconfraternity of Our Lady of Angels.
    Ditto, Rules.
    Christmas Offering (or 7s. 6d. a 1000).
    Devotions to S. Joseph.
    Explanation of the Medal or Cross of St. Benedict. 6s. per 100.
    Gospel according to St. John, *in Latin*. 1s. 6d. per 100.
    Indulgenced Prayers for Souls in Purgatory.
    Indulgenced Prayers for the Rosary of the Dead. 6s. per 100.
    Indulgenced Prayer before a Crucifix. 6s. per 100.
    Indulgences attached to Medals, Crosses, Statues, &c., by the Blessing of His Holiness and of those privileged to give his Blessing.
    Intentions for Indulgences.
    Litany of Our Lady of Angels.
    Litany of S. Joseph.
    Litany of Resignation.
    Litany of the Seven Dolours. 6s. per 100.
    Miraculous Prayer, August Queen of Angels.

Picture of Crucifixion, " I thirst " (or 7s. 6d. a 1000).
Prayer for One's Confessor.
Prayer to S. Philip Neri. 6s. per 100.
Prayers, to be said three days before and three days after Holy Communion. 6s. per 100.
Union of our Life with the Passion of our Lord by a daily Offering.
Visit to the Blessed Sacrament. 2s. 6d. per 100.

League of the Cross. By Fr. Richardson. 32mo., 1d.
LEBON (Hubert), Holy Communion—It is my Life! 12mo., 4s.
Legends of the Saints. By M. F. S. 16mo., 3s. 6d.
Lenten Thoughts. By Bishop Amherst. 18mo., 2s.; red edges, 2s. 6d.
Letters to my God-child. Letter IV. On the Veneration of the Blessed Virgin. By Mrs. Stuart Laidlaw. 16mo., 4d.
Letter to George Augustus Simcox. 8vo., 6d.
Life in the Cloister. By Miss Stewart. 12mo., 3s. 6d.
Life of Pleasure. By Mgr. Dechamps. 12mo., 1s. 6d.
Light of the Holy Spirit in the World. Five Sermons, by Bishop Hedley. 12mo., 1s.; cloth, 1s. 6d.
LIGUORI (S.), Fourteen Stations of the Cross. 18mo., 1d.
——— **Officium Parvum.** Latin and English. With Novena. 12mo., 1s.; cloth, 2s.; red edges, 3s.
——— **Selva**; or, a Collection of Matter for Sermons. 12mo., 5s.
——— **Way of Salvation.** 32mo., 1s.
Lily of S. Joseph: A little manual of Prayers and Hymns for Mass. 64mo., 2d.; cloth, 3d., 4d., and 6d.; gilt, 8d.; roan, 1s.; French morocco, 1s. 6d.; calf or morocco, 2s.; gilt, 2s. 6d.
Limerick Veteran; or, the Foster Sisters. *See* Stewart (Agnes M.).
Literature, Philosophy of, An Essay contributing to a. By B. A. M. 12mo., 6s.
Literature, Student's Handbook. *See* Jenkins (Rev. O. L.).
Little Hunchback. By Countess Ségur. 12mo., 3s.
Little Prayer Book. 32mo., 3d.
Lives of the First Religious of the Visitation of Holy Mary. By Mother Frances Magdalen de Chaugy. With 2 Photographs. 2 vols., 12mo., 10s.
Lost Children of Mount St. Bernard. 18mo., 6d.
Louis (St.), in Chains. Drama, Five Acts (Boys). 12mo., 2s.
Lourdes, Our Blessed Lady of. By Rev. Dr. Husenbeth. 18mo., 6d.; with the Novena, 1s.; cloth, 1s. 6d.
——— **Novena of**, for the use of the Sick. 4d.
——— **Litany of.** 1d. each.
——— **Photograph**, Carte de Visite, 1s.; Cabinet, 2s.; 4to., 4s.
Ludovic and Gertrude. By Conscience. 12mo., 4s.
LYONS (C. B.), Catholic Choir Manual. 12mo., 1s.
——— **Catholic Psalmist.** 12mo., 4s.   [18mo., 2s.
MACDANIEL (M. A.), Month of May for Interior Souls.
——— **Novena to S. Joseph.** 32mo., 4d.; cloth, 6d.
——— **Road to Heaven.** A Game. 3s. 6d.

R. Washbourne, 18 *Paternoster Row, London.*

MACEVILLY (Bishop), Exposition of the Epistles of St. Paul and of the Catholic Epistles. 2 vols., large 8vo. 18s.
———— Exposition of the Gospels. Large 8vo., Vol. I., 12s. 6d.
MACLEOD (Rev. X. D.), Devotion to Our Lady in North America. 8vo., 5s.
Major John Andre. An Historical Drama for Boys. Five Acts. 12mo., 2s.
MANNING (Cardinal), Church, Spirit and the Word. 8vo., 6d.
———— Confidence in God. 16mo., 1s.
———— Confraternity of the Holy Family. 8vo., 3d.
———— Convocation in Crown and Council. 8vo., 6d.
———— Glory of S. Vincent de Paul. 12mo., 1s.
———— Temporal Sovereignty of the Popes. 12mo., 1s.
MANNOCK (Patrick), Origin and Progress of Religious Orders, and Happiness of a Religious State. Translated from the Latin of Rev. F. Platus. 12mo., 2s. 6d.
Manual of Catholic Devotions. *See* Prayers, page 31.
Manual of Devotions in honour of Our Lady of Sorrows. Compiled by the Clergy at St. Patrick's, Soho. 18mo., 1s. 6d.
Manual of the Cross and Passion. *See* Passionist Fathers.
Manual of the Seven Dolours. *See* Passionist Fathers.
Manual of the Sisters of Charity. 18mo., 6s.
Margarethe Verflassen. Translated from the German by Mrs. Smith Sligo. 12mo., 1s. and 3s.; gilt, 3s. 6d.
Margaret Roper. By A. M. Stewart. 12mo., 6s.; extra, 7s.
MARQUIGNY (Pere), Life and Letters of Countess Adelstan. 12mo., 1s. and 2s. 6d.
MARSHALL (A. J. B., Esq.), Comedy of Convocation in the English Church. 8vo., 2s. 6d. *
———— English Religion. 8vo., 1s.
———— Infallibility of the Pope. 8vo., 1s. *
———— Oxford Undergraduate of Twenty Years Ago. 8vo., 2s. 6d.; cloth, 3s. 6d. *
———— Reply to the Bishop of Ripon's Attack on the Catholic Church. 8vo., 6d. *
MARSHALL (T. W. M., Esq.), Harmony of Anglicanism—Church Defence. 8vo., 2s. 6d. *
MARSHALL (Rev. W.), The Doctrine of Purgatory. 12mo., 1s.
MARTIN (Rev. E. R.), Rule of the Pope-King. 8vo., 6d.
Mary, A Remembrance of. 18mo., 2s.; roan, 3s.; calf, 4s. 6d.
Mary Christina of Savoy (Venerable). 18mo., 6d.
Mary Magdalen—A Homely Discourse. 12mo., 6d.
Mass, Descriptive Guide to. By Rev. Dr. Laing. 12mo., 1s., or stronger bound, 1s. 6d.
Mass, Devotions for. Very *Large type*, 18mo., 2d.
Mass, Life of our Lord in the. *See* Bagshawe (Bishop).

The 5 (*) *in one Volume*, 8vo., 6s.

R. Washbourne, 18 *Paternoster Row, London.*

Mass, Memorare. By Miss Cusack. 32mo., 2d.
Mass (The) a Devout Method. *See* Tronson.
Mass, A Devout Exposition of. *See* Rowley (Rev. A. J.).
Mathew (Father), Life of. By Miss Cusack. 12mo., 2s. 6d.
MAUREL (Rev. F. A.), Christian Instructed in the Nature and Use of Indulgences. 12mo., 3s.
Maxims of the Kingdom of Heaven. 12mo., 5s.; red edges, 5s. 6d.; calf or mor., 10s. 6d. Old Testament, 1s. 6d.; Gospels, 1s.
May, Month of, for all the Faithful. By Rev. P. Comerford. 32mo., 1s. [18mo., 2s.
May, Month of, for Interior Souls. By M. A. Macdaniel.
May, Month of, principally for the use of Religious Communities. 18mo., 1s. 6d.
May Readings for the Feasts of Our Lady. By Rev. A. P. Bethell. 18mo., 1s.; stronger bound, 1s. 6d.
M'CORRY (Rev. Dr.), Monks of Iona and the Duke of Argyll. 8vo., 3s. 6d.
———— Rome, Past, Present, Future. 8vo., 6d.
MEEHAN (M. H.), Fairy Tales for Little Children. 12mo., 1s.; stronger bound, 1s. 6d.; gilt, 2s.
MELIA (Rev. Dr.), Auricular Confession. 18mo., 1s. 6d.
Men and Women of the English Reformation from the days of Wolsey to the death of Cranmer. By S. H. Burke, M.A. 12mo., 2 Vols., 10s.; Vol. II., 5s.
MERMILLOD (Mgr.), The Supernatural Life. Translated from the French, with a Preface by Lady Herbert. 12mo., 5s.
M. F. S., Catherine Hamilton. 12mo., 2s. 6d.; gilt, 3s.
———— Catherine Grown Older. 12mo., 2s. 6d.; gilt, 3s.
———— Fluffy. A Tale for Boys. 12mo., 3s. 6d.
———— Legends of the Saints. 16mo., 3s. 6d.
———— Stories of Holy Lives. 12mo., 3s. 6d.
———— Stories of Martyr Priests. 12mo., 3s. 6d.
———— Stories of the Saints. 12mo., 3s. 6d.; gilt, 4s. 6d.
———————— Second Series. 12mo., 3s. 6d.; gilt, 4s. 6d.
———— Story of the Life of S. Paul. 12mo., 2s. 6d.
———— The Three Wishes. A Tale. 12mo., 2s. 6d.
———— Tom's Crucifix, and other Tales. 12mo., 3s.
Message from the Mother Heart of Mary. 18mo., 3d. and 6d.
MILES (G. H.), Truce of God. A Tale. 12mo., 4s.
MILNER (Bishop), Devotion to the Sacred Heart of Jesus. 32mo., 3d.; cloth, 6d.; gilt, 1s.
Miniature Prayer Book. *See* Prayers, page 31.
Miracles. A New Miracle at Rome, through the intercession of B. John Berchmans. 12mo., 2d.
———— Cure of Blindness, through the intercession of Our Lady and S. Ignatius. 12mo., 2d.
Mirror of Faith : your likeness in it. *See* Passionist Fathers.
Misgivings—Convictions. 12mo., 6d.
Missal. *See* Prayers, page 31.
Modern History and Biography, Lectures on. *See* Robertson.

R. Washbourne, 18 Paternoster Row, London.

Monastic Legends. By E. G. K. Browne. 8vo., 6d.
MONK (Rev. T. V.), Daily Exercises. *See* Prayers, page 30.
Monks of Iona and the Duke of Argyll. *See* M'Corry.
MONSABRE (Rev. Pere), Gold and Alloy. 12mo., 2s. 6d.
MONTAGU (Lord Robert), Civilization and the See of Rome. 8vo., 6d.
Montalembert (Count de). By George White. 12mo., 6d.
Mr. Vernon. A Novel. 8vo., 3 vols., 8s.; or in 1 vol., 7s. 6d.
MULHOLLAND (Rosa), Prince and Saviour : The Story of Jesus. 12mo., Coloured Illustrations, 2s. 6d.; 32mo., 6d.
Multiplication Table, on a sheet. 3s. per 100.
Munster Firesides. By E. Hall. 12mo., 3s. 6d.
MURRAY-LANE (Chevalier H.), Chronological Sketch of the Kings of England and the Kings of France. 12mo., 2s. 6d.; or in 2 vols., 1s. 6d. each.
MUSIC : Ave Maria, for Four Voices. By W. Schulthes. 1s. 3d.
    Cæcilian Society. *See* Separate List.
    Catholic Hymnal (English Words). For one, two, or four voices, with accompaniment. By Leopold de Prins. 4to., 2s.; bound, 3s.
    Cor Jesu, Salus in Te sperantium. By W. Schulthes, 2s.; with Harp Accompaniment, 2s. 6d.; abridged, 3d.
    Evening Hymn at the Oratory. By Rev. J. Nary. 3d.
    Hymns. By F. Faber. Large size. 9d. each. Pilgrims of the Night—O Paradise—True Shepherd—Sweet Saviour—Souls of Men—I come to Thee—O God, whose Thoughts—Jesus, my Lord—O come to the Merciful—How gently flow—Our Heavenly Father.
    Litanies (36) and Benediction Service. By W. Schulthes. 6s.
    Litanies (6). By E. Leslie. 6d.
    Litanies (18). By Rev. J. McCarthy. 1s. 3d.
    Mass of the Holy Child Jesus. By W. Schulthes. 3s. The vocal part only, 4d.; or 3s. per doz. Cloth, 6d.; or 4s. 6d. per doz.
    Ne projicias me a facie Tua. Motett for Four Voices. By W. Schulthes. 1s. 3d.
    Oratory Hymns. By W. Schulthes. 2 vols., 8s.
    Recordare. Oratorio Jeremiæ Prophetæ. By the same. 1s.
    Regina Cœli. Motett for Four Voices. By W. Schulthes. 3s. Vocal Arrangement, 1s.
    Twelve Latin Hymns. By W. Schulthes. 1s. 6d.
    Veni Domine. Motett for Four Voices. By W. Schulthes. 2s. Vocal Arrangement, 6d.
    Vespers and Benediction Service. Composed and harmonized by Leopold de Prins. 4to., 3s. 6d.
    ** *All the above (music) prices are nett.*
My Conversion and Vocation. By Rev. Father Schouvaloff, Barnabite. Translated from the French, with an Appendix, by Rev. C. Tondini. 12mo., 5s.

R. Washbourne, 18 Paternoster Row, London.

My Dream; and Verses Miscellaneous. *See* Herbert.
My Godmother's Stories from many Lands. By Mrs. T. K. Hervey. 12mo., 3s. 6d.
Mystical Flora of St. Francis de Sales. 4to., 8s.
NARY (Rev. J.) Evening Hymn at the Oratory. Music, 3d.
Nano Nangle; her Life, her Labours, &c. *See* Hutch.
Necessity of Enquiry as to Religion. *See* Pye (Henry John).
Ned Rusheen. By Miss Cusack. 12mo., 6s.
NEVIN (Willis, Esq.), The Jesuits, and other Essays. 12mo., 1s.; cloth, 2s. 6d.
NEWMAN (Rev. Dr.), Historical Sketches, 3 vols., 18s.; Miracles, 6s.; Discussions and Arguments, 6s.; Miscellanies, 6s.; Critical and Historical Essays, 2 vols., 12s.; Callista, 5s. 6d.; Arians, 6s.; Idea of a University, 7s.; Tracts, Theological and Ecclesiastical, 8s.; Loss and Gain, 5s. 6d.; Certain Difficulties felt by Anglicans, second series, 5s. 6d.
———— **Characteristics from the Writings of.** By W. S. Lilly. 12mo., 6s.
New Model for Youth; or, Life of Richard Aloysius Pennefather. By one of his Masters. 12mo., 3s. 6d.
New Testament (Rheims), with Annotations, References, and Index. 12mo., 2s. 6d. Illustrated, large 4to., 7s. 6d.
New Year's Gift to Our Heavenly Father. 32mo., 4d.
Nicholas; or, the Reward of a Good Action. 18mo., 6d.
NICHOLS (T. L.), Forty Years of American Life. 12mo., 5s. [18mo., 6d.
Nina and Pippo, the Lost Children of Mt. St. Bernard.
NOETHEN'S (Rev. T.), Good Thoughts for Priests and People; or, Short Meditations for every Day in the Year. 12mo., 8s.
———— **Compendium of the History of the Catholic Church.** 12mo., 8s.
Noethen's History of the Catholic Church. 12mo., 5s. 6d.
Novena to Our Blessed Lady of Lourdes for the use of the Sick. 18mo., 4d.
Novena of Meditations in honour of St. Joseph, according to the method of St. Ignatius, preceded by a new method of hearing Mass according to the intentions of the Souls in Purgatory. 18mo., 1s. 6d.
Nun's Advice to her Girls. By Miss Cusack. 12mo., 2s. 6d.
Occasional Prayers for Festivals. *See* Prayers, page 31.
O'CLERY (Keyes, M.P., K.S.G.), The History of the Italian Revolution. First Period—The Revolution of the Barricades (1796-1849). 8vo., 7s. 6d.
O'Connell: his Life and Times. *See* Cusack (M. F.).
O'Connell; his Speeches and Letters. *See* Cusack (M. F.).
O'Hagan (Mary), Abbess and Foundress of the Convent of the Poor Clares. By Miss Cusack. 8vo., 6s.
O'MAHONY (D.P.M.), Rome semper eadem. 8vo., 1s. 6d.

R. Washbourne, 18 Paternoster Row, London.

Oratorian Lives of the Saints. With Portrait, 12mo., 5s. a. vol
  I. S. Bernardine of Siena, Minor Observatine.
  II. S. Philip Benizi, Fifth General of the Servites.
  III. S. Veronica Giuliani, and B. Battista Varani.
  IV. S. John of God. By Canon Cianfogni.
Our Lady (Devotion to) in North America. *See* Macleod.
Our Lady's Lament. *See* Tame (C.E.).
Our Lady's Month. By Rev. A. P. Bethell. 18mo., 1s. and 1s. 6d.
Our Legends and Lives. By E. L. Hervey. 12mo., 6d.
Our Lord's Life, Passion, Death, and Resurrection. Translated from Ribadeneira. 12mo., 1s.
———— By Rev. H. Rutter. Illustrated. 12mo., 5s.
OXENHAM (H. N.), Dr. Pusey's Eirenicon considered in relation to Catholic Unity. 8vo., 6d.
———— **Poems.** 12mo., 3s. 6d.
Oxford Undergraduate of Twenty Years Ago. By a Bachelor of Arts. 8vo., 2s. 6d.; cloth, 3s. 6d.
OZANAM (A. F.), Protestantism and Liberty. Translated from the French by Wilfrid C. Robinson. 8vo., 1s.
Pale (The) and the Septs. A Romance of the Sixteenth Century. By Emelobie de Celtis. 2 vols., 12mo., 16s.
Panegyrics of Fr. Segneri, S.J. Translated from the original Italian. With a Preface, by Rev. W. Humphrey, S.J. 12mo., 5s.
Paradise of God; or the Virtues of the Sacred Heart. By Author of "God our Father," "Happiness of Heaven." 12mo., 4s.
Paray le Monial, and Bl. Margaret Mary. 18mo., 6d.
Passion of Our Lord, Harmony of. *See* Gayrard.
PASSIONIST FATHERS:—
  Christian Armed. 32mo., 1s. 6d.
  Guide to Sacred Eloquence. 18mo., 2s.
  Life of S. Paul of the Cross. 18mo., 3s.
  Manual of the Cross and Passion. 32mo., 3s.
  Manual of the Seven Dolours. 32mo., 1s. 6d.
  Mirror of Faith. 12mo., 3s.
  School of Jesus Crucified. 18mo., 5s.
Pastor and People. By Rev. T. J. Potter. 12mo., 5s.
Path (The) of Mary. By One of Her Loving Children. 12mo., 1s.
Path to Paradise. *See* Prayers, page 31.
Patrick (S.); the Apostle of Ireland. Who he was—where he came from—what he taught. 8vo., 1s.
Patrick (S.), Life of. 12mo., 1s.
Patrick's (S.) Manual. By Miss Cusack. 18mo., 3s. 6d.
Patron Saints. By E. A. Starr. Illustrated. 12mo., 10s.
Paul of the Cross (S.), Life of. *See* Passionist Fathers.
Penitential Psalms. *See* Blyth (Rev. F.).
PENS, Washbourne's Free and Easy. Fine, or Middle, or Broad Points, 1s. per gross.
People's Martyr. A Legend of Canterbury. 12mo., 4s.
Percy Grange. By Rev. T. J. Potter. 12mo., 3s.

Perpetual Adoration, Book of. Translated from the French of Mgr. Boudon; edited by Rev. Dr. Redman. 12mo., 3s. and 3s. 6d.
Peter (S.), his Name and his Office. See Allies (T. W., Esq., M.A.)
Peter, Years of. By an ex-Papal Zouave. 12mo., 1d.
Philip Benizi (S.), Life of. See Oratorian Lives of the Saints.
Philosophy, Elements of. By Rev. W. H. Hill. 8vo., 6s.
PHILPIN (Rev. F.), Holy Places; their sanctity and authenticity. With three Maps. 12mo., 2s. 6d. and 6s.
Photographs (10) illustrating the History of the Miraculous Hosts, called the Blessed Sacrament of the Miracle. 2s. 6d. the set.
Pilgrim's Way to Heaven. By Miss Cusack. 12mo., 4s. 6d.
Pius IX. 32mo., 6d.; 4to., 1d.
Plain Chant. See Gregorian.
——— The Cecilian Society Music kept in stock.
PLATUS (Rev. F.), Origin and Progress of Religious Orders, and Happiness of a Religious State. Translated by Patrick Mannock. 12mo., 2s. 6d.
PLAYS. See Dramas, page 10.
POIRIER (Bishop), A General Catechism of the Christian Doctrine. 18mo., 9d.
POOR CLARES OF KENMARE. See Cusack (Miss).
Pope-King, Rule of. By Rev. E. R. Martin. 8vo., 6d.
Pope of Rome. See Tondini (Rev. C.).
POTTER (Rev. T. J.), Extemporaneous Speaking. Sacred Eloquence. 12mo., 5s.
——— Farleyes of Farleye. 12mo., 2s. 6d.
——— Pastor and People. 12mo., 5s.
——— Percy Grange. 12mo., 3s.
——— Rupert Aubrey. 12mo., 3s.
——— Sir Humphrey's Trial. 16mo., 2s. 6d.
POWELL (J., Esq.), Two Years in the Pontifical Zouaves. Illustrated. 8vo., 3s. 6d.
PRADEL (Fr., O. P.), Life of St. Vincent Ferrer. Translated by Rev. Fr. Dixon. With a Photograph. 12mo., 5s.
PRAYER BOOKS. See page 30.
Prince and Saviour. See Mulholland (Rosa).
PRINS (Leopold de). See Music.
Pro-Cathedral, Kensington. Tinted View of the Interior, 11 × 15 inches, 1s.; Proofs, on larger paper, 2s.
Prophecies, Contemporary. By Mgr. Dupanloup. 8vo., 1s.
Protestantism and Liberty. See Robinson (W. C.).
Protestant Principles examined by the Written Word. 18mo., 1s.
Prussian Spy. A Novel. By V. Valmont. 12mo., 4s.
Psalmist, Catholic. By C. B. Lyons. 12mo., 4s.
Purgatory, A Novena in favour of the Souls in. 32mo., 3d.
Purgatory, The Doctrine of. By Rev. W. Marshall. 12mo, 1s.

Purgatory, Souls in. By Abbot Burder. 32mo., 3d.
Pusey's (Dr.) Eirenicon considered. *See* Oxenham (H. N.).
PYE (Henry John, M.A.), Necessity of Enquiry as to Religion. 32mo., 4d.; cloth, 6d.
RAM (Mrs. Abel), The Spiritual Life. Conferences, by Père Ravignan. 12mo., 5s.
RAMIERE (Rev. H.), Apostleship of Prayer. 12mo., 6s.
RAVIGNAN (Pere), The Spiritual Life, Conferences. Translated by Mrs. Abel Ram. 12mo., 5s.
Ravignan (Pere), Life of. 12mo., 9s.
RAWES (Rev F.), Homeward. 8vo., 2s.
—————— **Sursum.** 12mo., 1s.
Reading Lessons. By the Marist Brothers. Book 2. 18mo., 7d.
Recollections of the Reign of Terror. *See* Dumesnil (Abbé).
REDMAN (Rev. Dr.), Book of Perpetual Adoration. By Mgr. Boudon. 12mo., 3s.; red edges, 3s. 6d. 12mo., 1s.
REDMOND (Rev. Dr.), Eight Short Sermon Essays.
Reflections, One Hundred Pious. *See* Butler.
Regina Sæculorum; or, Mary Venerated in all Ages. Devotions to the Blessed Virgin from Ancient Sources. 12mo., 1s. and 3s.
Religious Orders. *See* Platus (Rev. F.).
Rest, on the Cross. By Eleanora Louisa Hervey. 12mo., 3s. 6d.
Reverse of the Medal. A Drama for Girls. 12mo., 6d.
RIBADENEIRA—Life, Passion, Death and Resurrection of our Lord. 12mo., 1s.
RICHARDSON (Rev. Fr.), Catholic Sick and Benefit Club; or, the Guild of our Lady; and St. Joseph's Catholic Burial Society. 32mo., 4d.
—————— **Catholic Total Abstinence League of the Cross.** 32mo., 1d.
—————— **Holy War.** Rules, ½d.; Crosses, 2d.
—————— **Little by Little**; or, the Penny Bank. 32mo., 1d.
—————— **S. Joseph's Catholic Burial Society.** 2d.
—————— **The Crusade**; or, Catholic Association for the Suppression of Drunkenness. 32mo., 1d.
Ritus Servandus in Expositione et Benedictione S.S. 4to., cloth, 5s. 6d.
Road to Heaven. A Game. By Miss M. A. Macdaniel. 3s. 6d.
ROBERTSON (Professor), Lectures on the Life, Writings, and Times of Edmund Burke. 12mo., 3s. 6d.
—————— **Anti-Janus.** By Hergenröther. 12mo., 6s.
—————— **Lectures on Modern History and Biography.** 12mo., 6s.
ROBINSON (Wilfrid C.), Protestantism and Liberty. Translated from the French of Professor Ozanam. 8vo., 1s.
Roman Question, The. By Rev. Dr. Husenbeth. 8vo., 6d.
—————— **and her Captors**: Letters collected and edited by Count Henri d'Ideville, and Translated by F. R. Wegg-Prosser. 12mo., 4s.

R. Washbourne, 18 *Paternoster Row, London.*

Rome, Past, Present, and Future. By Dr. M'Corry. 8vo., 6d
——— Personal Recollections of. By W. J. Jacob, 8vo., 6d.
——— semper eadem. By D. P. M. O'Mahony. 8vo., 1s. 6d.
———, The Victories of. By Rev. F. Beste. 8vo., 1s.
Rosalie; or, the Memoir of a French Child, told by herself. 12mo., 1s.; stronger bound, 1s. 6d.; gilt, 2s.
Rosary, Fifteen Mysteries of, and Fourteen Stations of the Cross. In One Volume, 32 Illustrations. 16mo., 1s. 6d.
Rosary for the Souls in Purgatory, with Indulgenced Prayer. 6d. and 9d. Medals separately, 1d. each, or 9s. gross. Prayers separately, 1d. each, 9d. a dozen, or 6s. for 100.
Rosary, Chats about the. *See* Aunt Margaret's Little Neighbours.
ROWLEY (Rev. Austin John), A Devout Exposition of the Holy Mass. Composed by John Heigham. 12mo., 4s.
Rupert Aubrey. By Rev. T. J. Potter. 12mo., 3s.
RUTTER (Rev. H.) Life and Sufferings of Our Lord, with Introduction by Rev. Dr. Husenbeth. Illustrated. 12mo., 5s.
Sacred Heart, Act of Consecration to. 1d.; or 6s. per 100.
——————————, Act of Reparation to. 1s. 2d. per 100.
——————————, Devotions to. By Rev. S. Franco. 12mo., 4s.; cheap edition, 2s.
——————————, Devotions to. By Bishop Milner. 32mo., 3d.; cloth, 6d.; gilt, 1s.
——————————, Devotions to. Translated by Rev. J. Joy Dean. 12mo., 3s.
——————————, Elevations to the. By Rev. Fr. Doyotte, S.J. 12mo., 3s.
——————————, Handbook of the Confraternity, for the use of Members. 18mo., 3d.
——————————, Little Treasury of. 32mo., 2s.; French morocco, 2s. 6d.; calf, 5s.; morocco, 6s.
——————————, Manual of Devotions to the, from the writings of Blessed Margaret Mary. 32mo., 3d.
—————————— offered to the Piety of the Young engaged in Study. By Rev. F. Deham. 32mo., 6d.
—————————— *See* Paradise of God.
—————————— Pleadings of. By Rev. M. Comerford. 18mo., 1s.; gilt edges, 2s.; with Handbook of the Confraternity, 1s. 6d.
——————————, Treasury of. 18mo., 3s. 6d.; roan, 4s. 6d.
Saints, Lives of. By Alban Butler. 4 vols., 8vo., 32s.; gilt, 48s.; and leather, gilt, 64s.; or the 4 vols. in 2, 28s.; gilt, 34s.
—————————— for every day in the Year. Beautifully printed, within borders from ancient sources, on thick toned paper. 4to., gilt, 16s.
——————— Patron. By E. A. Starr. Illustrated. 12mo., 10s.
Sanctuary Meditations for Priests and Frequent Communicants. Translated from the Spanish of Fr. Baltasar Gracian, by Mariana Monteiro. 12mo., 4s.
SCARAMELLI—Directorium Asceticum; or, Guide to the Spiritual Life. 4 vols. 12mo., 24s.

R. Washbourne, 18 *Paternoster Row, London.*

SCHMID (Canon), Tales. Illustrated. 12mo., 3s. 6d. Separately:—The Canary Bird, The Dove, The Inundation, The Rose Tree, The Water Jug, The Wooden Cross. 6d. each; gilt, 1s.
SCHOOL BOOKS. Supplied according to order.
School of Jesus Crucified. By the Passionist Fathers. 18mo., 5s.
SCHOUVALOFF (Rev. Father, Barnabite), My Conversion and Vocation. Translated from the French, with an Appendix, by Fr. C. Tondini. 12mo., 5s.
SCHULTHES (William). *See* Music.
Scraps from my Scrapbook. *See* Arnold (M. J.).
SEGNERI (Fr., S.J.), Panegyrics. Translated from the original Italian. With a Preface, by Rev. W. Humphrey, of the same Society. 12mo., 5s.
SEGUR (Mgr.), Books for Little Children. Translated. 32mo., 3d. each. Confession, Holy Communion, Child Jesus, Piety, Prayer, Temptation and Sin. In one volume, cloth, 2s.
────── Practical Counsels for Holy Communion. 18mo., 9d.
Segur (Countess de), The Little Hunchback. 12mo., 3s.
Seigneret (Paul), Life of. 12mo., 6d., 1s., and 1s. 6d.; gilt, 2s.
Selva; a Collection of Matter for Sermons. By St. Liguori. 12mo., 5s.
Semi-Tropical Trifles. By H. Compton. 12mo., 1s.; cloth, 2s. 6d.
Sermon Essays. By Rev. Dr. Redmond. 12mo., 1s.
Sermons. By Dr. Husenbeth. 8vo., 6d. each. 1. Lady Bedingfield. 2. Hon. Mary Stafford Jerningham. 3. Right Hon. George Lord Stafford. 4. Hon. Edwin Stafford Jerningham.
────── By Father Burke, O.P., and others. 12mo., 2s.
────── The Light of the Holy Spirit in the World. By Bishop Hedley. 1s.; cloth, 1s. 6d.
────── One Hundred Short. By Rev. Fr. Thomas. 8vo., 12s.
Serving Boy's Manual, and Book of Public Devotions. Containing all those prayers and devotions for Sundays and Holydays, usually divided in their recitation between the Priest and the Congregation. Compiled from approved sources, and adapted to Churches, served either by the Secular or Regular Clergy. 32mo., embossed, 1s.; French morocco, 2s.; calf, 4s.; with Epistles and Gospels, 6d. extra.
Seven Sacraments Explained and Defended. 18mo., 1s. 6d.
SHAKESPEARE. Expurgated edition. By Rosa Baughan. 8vo., 6s. The Comedies only, 3s. 6d.
Shandy Maguire. A Farce for Boys. 12mo., 1s.
Siege of Limerick (Florence O'Neill). *See* Stewart (Agnes M.).
SIGHART (Dr.) Albert the Great. *See* Albert.
Silver Teapot. By Elizabeth King. 18mo., 4d.
Simple Tales—Waiting for Father, &c., &c. 16mo., 2s. 6d.
Sir Ælfric and other Tales. *See* Bampfield (Rev. G.).
Sir Humphrey's Trial. By Rev. T. J. Potter. 16mo., 2s. 6d.
Sir Thomas Maxwell and his Ward. By Miss Bridges, 12mo, 1s. and 2s.
Sir Thomas More. *See* Stewart (A. M.).
Sisters of Charity, Manual of. 18mo. 6s.

R. Washbourne, 18 *Paternoster Row, London.*

SMITH-SLIGO (A. V., Esq.), Life of the Ven. Anna Maria Taigi. Translated from the French of Calixte. 8vo., 2s. 6d. and 5s. [3s. 6d.
────── (Mrs.) Margarethe Verflassen. 12mo., 1s., 3s., and
Soul (The), United to Jesus in the Adorable Sacrament. 32mo., 1s. 6d.
SPALDING'S (Abp.) Works. 5 vols., 52s. 6d.; or separately: Evidences of Catholicity, 10s. 6d.; Miscellanea, 2 vols., 21s.; Protestant Reformation, 2 vols., 21s.
Spalding (Archbishop), Life of. 8vo., 10s. 6d.
Spalding (Abp.). Sermon at the Month's Mind. 8vo., 1s.
Spiritual Conferences on the Mysteries of Faith and the Interior Life. By Father Collins. 12mo., 5s.
Spiritual Life. Conferences by Père Ravignan. Translated by Mrs. Abel Ram. 12mo., 5s.
Spiritual Works of Louis of Blois. Edited by Rev. F. John Bowden. 12mo., 3s. 6d.; red edges, 4s.
STARR (Eliza Allen), Patron Saints. Illustrated. 12mo., 10s.
Stations of the Cross, Devotions for Public and Private Use at the. By Miss Cusack. Illustrated. 16mo., 1s. and 1s. 6d.
Stations of the Cross. By S. Liguori. 18mo., 1d.
Stephen Langton, Life of. 12mo., 2s. 6d.
STEWART (A. M.), Alone in the World. 12mo., 4s. 6d.
────── St. Angela's Manual. *See* Angela (S.)
────── Biographical Readings. 12mo., 4s. 6d.
────── Florence O'Neill, the Rose of St. Germains; or, the Days of the Siege of Limerick. 12mo., 5s.; extra, 6s.
────── General Questions in History, Chronology, Geography, the Arts, &c. 12mo., 4s. 6d.
────── Life and Letters of Sir Thomas More. Illustrated, 10s. 6d.; gilt, 11s. 6d.
────── Life of S. Angela Merici. 12mo., 4s. 6d.
────── Life in the Cloister. 12mo., 3s. 6d. [extra, 6s.
────── Limerick Veteran; or, the Foster Sisters. 12mo., 5s.;
────── Margaret Roper. 12mo., 6s.; extra, 7s.
Stories for my Children—The Angels and the Sacraments. 16mo., 1s.
Stories of Holy Lives. By M. F. S., Author of "Stories of the Saints," "Tom's Crucifix, and other Tales," &c. 12mo., 3s.6d.
Stories of Martyr Priests. By M. F. S. 12mo., 3s. 6d.
Stories of the Saints. By M. F. S. 12mo., 1st Series, 3s. 6d.; gilt, 4s. 6d. 2nd Series, 3s. 6d.; gilt, 4s. 6d.
Stormsworth, with other Poems and Plays. By the author of "Thy Gods, O Israel.' 12mo., 3s. 6d.
Story of Marie and other Tales. 12mo., 2s.; gilt, 3s.; or separately:—The Story of Marie, 2d.; Nelly Blane, and a Contrast, 2d.; A Conversion and a Death-bed, 2d.; Herbert Montagu, 2d.; Jane Murphy, the Dying Gipsy, and the Nameless Grave, 2d.; The Beggars, and True and False Riches, 2d.; Pat and his Friend, 2d.

R. Washbourne, 18 *Paternoster Row, London.*

Story of the Life of St. Paul. By M. F. S., author of "Stories of the Saints." 12mo., 2s. 6d.

Sufferings of our Lord. Sermons preached by Father Claude de la Colombière, S.J., in the Chapel Royal, St. James's, in the year 1677. 18mo., 1s.; stronger bound, 1s. 6d.; red edges, 2s.

Supernatural Life, The. By Mgr. Mermillod. Translated from the French, with a Preface by Lady Herbert. 12mo., 5s.

Supremacy of the Roman See. By C. E. Tame, Esq. 8vo., 6d.

Sure Way to Heaven. A Little Manual for Confession and Holy Communion. 32mo., 6d.; Persian, 2s. 6d.; calf or morocco, 3s. 6d.

Sweetness of Holy Living; or, Honey culled from the Flower Garden of S. Francis of Sales. 18mo., 1s.; French morocco, 3s.

Taigi (Anna Maria), Life of. Translated from the French of Calixte by A. V. Smith-Sligo, Esq. 8vo., 2s. 6d. and 5s.

Tales and Sketches. *See* Fleet.

TAME (C. E., Esq.), Early English Literature. 16mo., 2s. a vol. I. Our Lady's Lament, and the Lamentation of S. Mary Magdalene. II. Life of Our Lady, in verse.

—————— **Supremacy of the Roman See.** 8vo., 6d.

TANDY (Rev. Dr.), Terry O'Flinn. 12mo., 1s.; stronger bound, 1s. 6d.; gilt, 2s.

TAUNTON (M.), Last of the Catholic O'Malleys. 18mo., 1s. 6d.; stronger bound, 2s.

—————— **One Hundred Pious Reflections**, from Alban Butler's Lives of the Saints. 18mo., 1s.; stronger bound, 2s.

Temperance Books. *See* Richardson (Rev. Fr.).

—————— Cards (Illuminated), 3d. each. [3d. each.

—————— Medals—Immaculate Conception, St. Patrick, St. Joseph.

Terry O'Flinn. By Rev. Dr. Tandy. 12mo., 1s.; stronger bound, 1s. 6d.; gilt, 2s.

Testimony; or, the Necessity of Enquiry as to Religion. By John Henry Pye, M.A. 32mo., 4d.; cloth, 6d.

THOMAS (H. J.), One Hundred Short Sermons. 8vo., 12s.

Three Wishes. A Tale. By M. F. S. 12mo., 2s. 6d.

Threshold of the Catholic Church. *See* Bagshawe.

Tom's Crucifix, and other Tales. By M. F. S. 12mo., 3s.

TONDINI (Rev. Cæsarius), My Conversion and Vocation. By Rev. Fr. Schouvaloff. 12mo., 5s.

—————— **The Pope of Rome and the Popes of the Oriental Orthodox Church.** An essay on Monarchy in the Church, with special reference to Russia, from original documents, Russian and Greek. Second Edition. 12mo., 3s. 6d.

—————— **Some Documents concerning of the Association Prayers in Honour of Mary Immaculate, for the Return of the Greek-Russian Church to Catholic Unity.** 12mo., 3d.

Trials of Faith. *See* Browne (E. G. K.).

TRONSON (Abbe), The Mass: a devout Method of assisting at it. 32mo., 4d.

R. Washbourne, 18 Paternoster Row, London.

Truce of God. A Tale of the XI. Century. *See* Miles (G. H.).
Two Colonels. By Father Thomas. 12mo., 6s.
Ursuline Manual. *See* Prayers, page 32.
VALMONT (V.), The Prussian Spy. A Novel. 12mo., 4s.
Veronica Giuliani (S.), Life of, and B. Battista Varani. With a Photographic Portrait. 12mo., 5s.
Village Innkeeper. By Conscience. 12mo., 4s.
Village Lily. A Tale. 12mo., 1s.; gilt, 1s. 6d.
Vincent Ferrer (S.), of the Order of Friar Preachers; his Life, Spiritual Teaching, and Practical Devotion. By Rev. Fr. Andrew Pradel, O.P. Translated from the French by the Rev. Fr. T. A. Dixon, O.P., with a Photograph. 12mo., 5s.
VINCENT OF LIRINS (S.). A Translation of the Commonitory of S. Vincent of Lirins. 12mo., 1s. 3d.
Vincent of Paul (S.), Glory of. *See* Manning (Archbishop).
VIRGIL. Literally translated by Davidson. 12mo., 2s. 6d.
"Vitis Mystica"; or, the True Vine. *See* Brownlow.
WALLER (J. F., Esq.), Festival Tales. 12mo., 5s.
WALSH (W. H., Esq.), Henry V. 8vo., 6d.
Way of Salvation. By S. Liguori. 32mo., 1s.
Weedall (Mgr.), Life of. By Rev. Dr. Husenbeth. 8vo., 1s.
WEGG-PROSSER (F. R.), Rome and her Captors. 12mo., 4s.
What is Christianity? By Rev. F. H. Laing, D.D. 12mo., 6d.
Whence the Monarch's Right to Rule? *See* Laing (Rev. D.).
WHITE (George), Cardinal Wiseman. 12mo., 1s. and 1s. 6d.
——— Comte de Montalembert. 12mo., 6d.
——— Life of S. Edmund of Canterbury. 1s. and 1s. 6d.
——— Map of London, Showing the Churches. 6d.
WHITELOCK (A.), The Chances of War. An Irish Tale. 8vo., 5s.
William (St.), of York. A Drama in Two Acts. (Boys.) 12mo., 6d.
WILLIAMS (Canon), Anglican Orders. 12mo., 3s. 6d.
Wiseman (Cardinal), Life and Obsequies. 12mo., 1s. and 1s. 6d.
——— Recollections of. By M. J. Arnold. 12mo., 2s. 6d.
Woman's Work in Modern Society. *See* Cusack (M. F.)
WOODS (Canon), Defence of the Roman Church against F. Gratry. Translated from the French of Gueranger. 8vo., 1s. 6d.
WYATT-EDGELL (Alfred), Stormsworth, with other Poems and Plays. 12mo., 2s. 6d.
——— Thy Gods! O Israel. 12mo., 2s.
Young Catholic's Guide to Confession and Holy Communion. By Dr. Kenny. 32mo., 4d.; cloth, 6d.; red edges, 9d.; French morocco, 1s. 6d.; calf or morocco, 2s. 6d.
Young Doctor. By Conscience. 12mo., 4s.
YOUNG (T., Esq.), History of Ireland. 18mo., 2s. 6d.
Zouaves, Pontifical, Two Years in. By Joseph Powell, Z.P. Illustrated. 8vo., 3s. 6d.

R. Washbourne, 18 Paternoster Row London.

PRAYER BOOKS.

Garden, Little, of the Soul. Edited by the Rev. R. G. Davis. *With Imprimatur of the Archbishop of Westminster.* This book, as its name imports, contains a selection from the "Garden of the Soul" of the Prayers and Devotions of most general use. Whilst it will serve as a *Pocket Prayer Book* for all, it is, by its low price, *par excellence*, the Prayer Book for children and for the very poor. In it are to be found the old familiar Devotions of the "Garden of the Soul," as well as many important additions, such as the Devotions to the Sacred Heart, to Saint Joseph, to the Guardian Angels, and others. The omissions are mainly the Forms of administering the Sacraments, and Devotions that are not of very general use. It is printed in a clear type, on a good paper, both especially selected, for the purpose of obviating the disagreeableness of small type and inferior paper. Tenth thousand.

32mo., price, cloth, 6d.; with rims, 1s. Embossed, red edges, 9d.; with rims and clasp, 1s. 3d.; Strong roan, 1s.; with rims and classs 1s. 6d. French morocco, 1s. 6d.; with rims and clasp, 2s. French morocco extra gilt, 2s.; with rims and clasp, 2s. 6d. Calf or morocco, 3s.; with rims and clasp, 4s. Calf or morocco, extra gilt, 4s.; with rims and clasp, 5s. Morocco antique, 7s. 6d., 10s. 6d., 12s., 16s. Velvet, rims and clasp, 5s., 8s. 6d., and 10s. 6d. Russia, 5s.; with clasp, &c., 8s.; Russia antique, 17s. 6d. Ivory, with rims and clasp, 10s. 6d., 13s., 15s., 17s. 6d. Imitation ivory, with rims and clasp, 3s. With oxydized silver or gilt mountings, in morocco case, 25s.

Catholic Hours: a Manual of Prayer, including Mass and Vespers. By J. R. Digby Beste, Esq. 32mo., cloth, 2s.; red edges, 2s. 6d.; roan, 3s.; morocco, 6s.

Catholic Piety; or, Key of Heaven, with Epistles and Gospels. Large 32mo., roan, 1s. 6d. and 2s.; French morocco, with rims and clasp, 2s. 6d.; extra gilt, 3s.; with rims and clasp, 3s. 6d.; velvet, 3s. 6d. and 10s.

Catholic Piety; or, Key of Heaven. 32mo., 6d.; rims and clasp, 1s.; French morocco, 1s.; velvet, with rims and clasp, 2s. 6d.; with Epistles and Gospels, roan, 1s.; French morocco, 1s. 6d.; with rims and clasp, 2s.; extra gilt, 2s.; Persian, 2s. 6d.; imitation ivory, 3s.; morocco, 3s. 6d.; velvet, rims and clasp, 3s. 6d.

Crown of Jesus. 18mo., Persian calf, 6s. Calf or Morocco, 7s. 6d. and 8s. 6d.; with rims and clasp, 10s. 6d. Calf or morocco, extra gilt, 10s. 6d.; with rims and clasp, 12s. 6d; with turn-over edges, 10s. 6d. Ivory, with rims and clasp, 21s., 25s., 27s. 6d. and 30s.

Devotions for Mass. Very large type, 12mo., 2d.

Daily Exercises for Devout Christians, in which are contained various practices of piety tending to a Holy Life and a Happy Death. By Rev. T. V. Monk, O.S.B. Edited by a Carmelite Father. 18mo., 4s., better bound, 5s., 6s. 6d., 9s., 10s. 6d., 12s. 6d.

Garden of the Soul. Very large Type. 18mo., cloth, 1s.; with Epistles and Gospels, 1s. 6d.; French morocco, 2s. 6d.; with E. and G., 3s. 6d. Best edition, without E. and G., 3s. 6d. and 7s. 6d. Epistles and Gospels, in French morocco, 2s.

R. Washbourne, 18 *Paternoster Row, London.*

Holy Childhood. Simple Prayers for very little children. 32mo., 1s.; gilt, 1s. 6d.
Illustrated Manual of Prayers. 32mo., 3d.; cloth, 4d.
Key of Heaven. *Very large type..* 18mo., 1s.; leather, 2s. 6d.; extra gilt, 3s.
Lily of St. Joseph, The; a little Manual of Prayers and Hymns for Mass. 64mo., price 2d.; cloth, 3d., 4d., 6d., or 8d.; roan, 1s.; French morocco, 1s. 6d.; calf or morocco, 2s.; gilt, 2s. 6d.
Little Prayer Book, The, for Ordinary Catholic Devotions. 32mo., cloth, 3d.
Manual of Catholic Devotions. Small, for the waistcoat pocket. 64mo., 6d.; with Epistles and Gospels, cloth, rims, 1s.; roan, 1s.; with tuck, 1s. 6d.; calf or morocco, 2s. 6d. Imitation Ivory, 2s.
Manual of the Sisters of Charity. 18mo., 6s.
Memorare Mass. By the Poor Clares of Kenmare. 32mo., 2d.
Miniature Prayer Book, 48mo., 6d.; cape, 1s. calf, 2s. 6d.; imitation ivory, rims and clasp, 3s.; morocco, rims and clasp, 4s. 6d.; with tuck, 4s. 6d.; velvet, with rims and clasp, 4s. 6d.; ivory, with clasp, 7s. 6d.; russia, with clasp, 10s. 6d.
Missal (Complete). 18mo., Persian, 8s. 6d.; calf or morocco, 10s. 6d.; with rims and clasp, 13s. 6d.; calf or mor., extra gilt, 12s. 6d., with rims and clasp, 15s. 6d.; morocco, with turn-over edges, 13s. 6d.; morocco antique, 15s.; velvet, 20s.; Russia, 20s.; ivory, with rims and clasp, 31s. 6d. and 35s.
——— A very beautiful edition, handsomely bound in morocco, gilt mountings, silk linings, edges red on gold, in a morocco case. Illustrated, £5. [clasp, 8s.
Missal and Vesper Book, in one vol. 32mo., morocco, 6s.; with
Occasional Prayers for Festivals. By Rev. T. Barge. 32mo., 4d. and 6d.; gilt, 1s.
Path to Paradise. 32 full-page Illustrations. 32mo., cloth, 3d. With 50 Illustrations, cloth, 4d. Superior edition, 6d. and 1s.
Serving Boy's Manual and Book of Catholic Devotions, containing all those Prayers and Devotions for Sundays and Holidays, usually divided in their recitation between the Priest and the Congregation. Compiled from approved sources, and adapted to Churches served either by the Secular or the Regular Clergy. 32mo., Embossed, 1s.; with Epistles and Gospels, 1s. 6d.; French morocco, 2s., with Epistles and Gospels, 2s. 6d.; calf, 4s., with Epistles and Gospels, 4s. 6d.
S. Patrick's Manual. Compiled by Sister Mary Frances Clare. 18mo., 3s. 6d.
Sure Way to Heaven. 32mo., cloth, 6d.: Persian, 2s. 6d.; calf or morocco, 3s. 6d.
Treasury of the Sacred Heart. 18mo., 3s. 6d.; roan, 4s. 6d. 32mo., 2s.; French morocco, 2s. 6d.; calf 5s.; morocco, 6s.
Ursuline Manual. 18mo., 4s.; Persian calf, 7s. 6d.; morocco, 10s.

Garden of the Soul. (WASHBOURNE'S EDITION.) Edited by the Rev. R. G. Davis. *With Imprimatur of the Archbishop of Westminster.* Thirteenth Thousand. This Edition retains all the Devotions that have made the GARDEN OF THE SOUL, now for many generations, the well-known Prayer-book for English Catholics. During many years various Devotions have been introduced, and, in the form of appendices, have been added to other editions. These have now been incorporated into the body of the work, and, together with the Devotions to the Sacred Heart, to Saint Joseph, to the Guardian Angels, the Itinerarium, and other important additions, render this edition pre-eminently the Manual of Prayer, for both public and private use. The version of the Psalms has been carefully revised, and strictly conformed to the Douay translation of the Bible, published with the approbation of the LATE CARDINAL WISEMAN. The Forms of administering the Sacraments have been carefully translated, *as also the rubrical directions,* from the Ordo Administrandi Sacramenta. To enable all present, either at baptisms or other public administrations of the Sacraments, to pay due attention to the sacred rites, the Forms are inserted without any curtailment, both in Latin and English. The Devotions at Mass have been carefully revised, and enriched by copious adaptations from the prayers of the Missal. The preparation for the Sacraments of Penance and the Holy Eucharist have been the objects of especial care, to adapt them to the wants of those whose religious instruction may be deficient. Great attention has been paid to the quality of the paper and to the size of type used in the printing, to obviate that weariness so distressing to the eyes, caused by the use of books printed in small close type and on inferior paper.

32mo. Embossed, 1s.; with rims and clasp, 1s. 6d.; with Epistles and Gospels, 1s. 6d.; with rims and clasp, 2s. French morocco, 2s.; with rims and clasp, 2s. 6d.; with E. and G., 2s. 6d.; with rims and clasp, 3s. French morocco extra gilt, 2s. 6d.; with rims and clasp, 3s.; with E. and G., 3s.; with rims and clasp, 3s. 6d. Calf, or morocco 4s.; with rims and clasp, 5s. 6d.; with E. and G., 4s. 6d., with rims and clasp, 6s. Calf or morocco extra gilt, 5s.; with rims and clasp, 6s. 6d.; with E. and G., 5s. 6d.; with rims and clasp, 7s. Velvet, with rims and clasp, 7s. 6d., 10s. 6d., and 13s.; with E. and G., 8s., 11s., and 13s. 6d. Russia, antique, with clasp, 10s., 12s. 6d.; with E. and G., 10s. 6d., 13s., with corners and clasps, 20s.; with E. and G., 20s. 6d. Ivory, 14s., 16s., 20s., and 22s. 6d.; with E. and G., 14s. 6d.; 16s. 6d., 20s. 6d., and 23s. Morocco antique, 10s., with 2 patent clasps, 12s.; with E. and G., 10s. 6d. and 12s. 6d.; with corners and clasps, 18s.; with E. and G., 18s 6d.

The Epistles and Gospels, in cloth, 6d.; roan, 1s. 6d.

' This is one of the best editions we have seen of one of the best of all our Prayer Books. It is well printed in clear, large type, on good paper."—*Catholic Opinion*
"A very complete arrangement of this which is emphatically the Prayer Book of every Catholic household. It is as cheap as it is good, and we heartily recommend it."—*Universe.* "Two striking features are the admirable order displayed throughout the book, and the insertion of the Indulgences in small type above Indulgenced Prayers. In the Devotions for Mass, the editor has, with great discrimination, drawn largely on the Church's Prayers, as given us in the Missal."—*Weekly Register.*

R. *Washbourne,* 18 *Paternoster Row, London.*

Purgatory, Souls in. By Abbot Burder. 32mo., 3d.
Pusey's (Dr.) Eirenicon considered. *See* Oxenham (H. N.).
PYE (Henry John, M.A.), Necessity of Enquiry as to Religion. 32mo., 4d.; cloth, 6d.
RAM (Mrs. Abel), The Spiritual Life. Conferences, by Père Ravignan. 12mo., 5s.
RAMIERE (Rev. H.), Apostleship of Prayer. 12mo., 6s.
RAVIGNAN (Pere), The Spiritual Life, Conferences. Translated by Mrs. Abel Ram. 12mo., 5s.
Ravignan (Pere), Life of. 12mo., 9s.
RAWES (Rev F.), Homeward. 8vo., 2s.
——— **Sursum.** 12mo., 1s.
Reading Lessons. By the Marist Brothers. Book 2. 18mo., 7d.
Recollections of the Reign of Terror. *See* Dumesnil (Abbé).
REDMAN (Rev. Dr.), Book of Perpetual Adoration. By Mgr. Boudon. 12mo., 3s.; red edges, 3s. 6d.
12mo., 1s.
REDMOND (Rev. Dr.), Eight Short Sermon Essays.
Reflections, One Hundred Pious. *See* Butler.
Regina Sæculorum; or, Mary Venerated in all Ages. Devotions to the Blessed Virgin from Ancient Sources. 12mo., 1s. and 3s.
Religious Orders. *See* Platus (Rev. F.).
Rest, on the Cross. By Eleanora Louisa Hervey. 12mo., 3s. 6d.
Reverse of the Medal. A Drama for Girls. 12mo., 6d.
RIBADENEIRA—Life, Passion, Death and Resurrection of our Lord. 12mo., 1s.
RICHARDSON (Rev. Fr.), Catholic Sick and Benefit Club; or, the Guild of our Lady; and St. Joseph's Catholic Burial Society. 32mo., 4d.
——— **Catholic Total Abstinence League of the Cross.** 32mo., 1d.
——— **Holy War.** Rules, ½d.; Crosses, 2d.
——— **Little by Little**; or, the Penny Bank. 32mo., 1d.
——— **S. Joseph's Catholic Burial Society.** 2d.
——— **The Crusade**; or, Catholic Association for the Suppression of Drunkenness. 32mo., 1d.
Ritus Servandus in Expositione et Benedictione S.S. 4to., cloth, 5s. 6d.
Road to Heaven. A Game. By Miss M. A. Macdaniel. 3s. 6d.
ROBERTSON (Professor), Lectures on the Life, Writings, and Times of Edmund Burke. 12mo., 3s. 6d.
——— **Anti-Janus.** By Hergenröther. 12mo., 6s.
——— **Lectures on Modern History and Biography.** 12mo., 6s.
ROBINSON (Wilfrid C.), Protestantism and Liberty. Translated from the French of Professor Ozanam. 8vo., 1s.
Roman Question, The. By Rev. Dr. Husenbeth. 8vo., 6d.
——— **and her Captors**: Letters collected and edited by Count Henri d'Ideville, and Translated by F. R. Wegg-Prosser. 12mo., 4s.

R. Washbourne, 18 Paternoster Row, London.

Rome, Past, Present, and Future. By Dr. M'Corry. 8vo., 6d
——— Personal Recollections of. By W. J. Jacob, 8vo., 6d.
——— semper eadem. By D. P. M. O'Mahony. 8vo., 1s. 6d.
———, The Victories of. By Rev. F. Beste. 8vo., 1s.
Rosalie; or, the Memoir of a French Child, told by herself. 12mo., 1s.; stronger bound, 1s. 6d.; gilt, 2s.
Rosary, Fifteen Mysteries of, and Fourteen Stations of the Cross. In One Volume, 32 Illustrations. 16mo., 1s. 6d.
Rosary for the Souls in Purgatory, with Indulgenced Prayer. 6d. and 9d. Medals separately, 1d. each, or 9s. gross. Prayers separately, 1d. each, 9d. a dozen, or 6s. for 100.
Rosary, Chats about the. *See* Aunt Margaret's Little Neighbours.
ROWLEY (Rev. Austin John), A Devout Exposition of the Holy Mass. Composed by John Heigham. 12mo., 4s.
Rupert Aubrey. By Rev. T. J. Potter. 12mo., 3s.
RUTTER (Rev. H.) Life and Sufferings of Our Lord, with Introduction by Rev. Dr. Husenbeth. Illustrated. 12mo., 5s.
Sacred Heart, Act of Consecration to. 1d.; or 6s. per 100.
——————————, Act of Reparation to. 1s. 2d. per 100.
——————————, Devotions to. By Rev. S. Franco. 12mo., 4s.; cheap edition, 2s.
——————————, Devotions to. By Bishop Milner. 32mo., 3d.; cloth, 6d.; gilt, 1s.
——————————, Devotions to. Translated by Rev. J. Joy Dean. 12mo., 3s.
——————————, Elevations to the. By Rev. Fr. Doyotte, S.J. 12mo., 3s.
——————————, Handbook of the Confraternity, for the use of Members. 18mo., 3d.
——————————, Little Treasury of. 32mo., 2s.; French morocco, 2s. 6d.; calf, 5s.; morocco, 6s.
——————————, Manual of Devotions to the, from the writings of Blessed Margaret Mary. 32mo., 3d.
—————————— offered to the Piety of the Young engaged in Study. By Rev. F. Deham. 32mo., 6d.
—————————— *See* Paradise of God.
——————————, Pleadings of. By Rev. M. Comerford. 18mo., 1s.; gilt edges, 2s.; with Handbook of the Confraternity, 1s. 6d.
——————————, Treasury of. 18mo., 3s. 6d.; roan, 4s. 6d.
Saints, Lives of. By Alban Butler. 4 vols., 8vo., 32s.; gilt, 48s.; and leather, gilt, 64s.; or the 4 vols. in 2, 28s.; gilt, 34s.
————————————— for every day in the Year. Beautifully printed, within borders from ancient sources, on thick toned paper. 4to., gilt, 16s.
———————— Patron. By E. A. Starr. Illustrated. 12mo., 10s.
Sanctuary Meditations for Priests and Frequent Communicants. Translated from the Spanish of Fr. Baltasar Gracian, by Mariana Monteiro. 12mo., 4s.
SCARAMELLI—Directorium Asceticum; or, Guide to the Spiritual Life. 4 vols. 12mo., 24s.

R. Washbourne, 18 Paternoster Row, London.

www.ingramcontent.com/pod-product-compliance
Lightning Source LLC
Chambersburg PA
CBHW030015240426
43672CB00007B/955